essential
astrology

essential astrology

**LEARN TO BE YOUR OWN ASTROLOGER AND
UNLOCK THE SECRETS OF THE SIGNS AND PLANETS**

Joanna Watters

CICO BOOKS
LONDON NEW YORK

This book is dedicated to Paul Hitchings and Ronnie Lloyd whose combined worldly and spiritual wisdom has seen me through every challenge of my life and taught me so much over the last 30 years. Without you my work would lack the depth that I hope I have achieved and I dedicate this book to both of you with all my love and gratitude.

This edition published in 2023 by CICO Books
An imprint of Ryland Peters & Small Ltd
20–21 Jockey's Fields   341 E 116th St
London, WC1R 4BW   New York, NY 10029

www.rylandpeters.com

10 9 8 7 6 5 4 3 2 1

First published in 2015 as *Be Your Own Astrologer*.

A CIP catalog record for this book is available from the Library of Congress and the British Library.

ISBN: 978 1 80065 235 4

Printed in China

Editor: Jennifer Jahn
Designer: Emily Breen
Illustrator: Sarah Perkins

In-house editor: Dawn Bates
Art director: Sally Powell
Head of production: Patricia Harrington
Publishing manager: Penny Craig
Publisher: Cindy Richards

CONTENTS

INTRODUCTION

The road to astrology is paved with misconceptions, which are largely down to the fact that the gap between Sun-sign astrology and horoscopy is immense. Whilst the former is kept alive and kicking in media horoscopes, often referred to as "Your Stars," the latter is the study of the individual horoscope, also known as the birth chart or the nativity. Your stars in a newspaper, magazine, or on a website are not in fact your "horoscope," but an astrologer's "take" on the current planetary activity. Even when written professionally, such columns can only generalize, they still wear the fortune teller's hat and are inevitably branded in the public eye as entertainment. On the other hand, the study of your own birth chart means unlocking a treasure trove of self awareness, guidance, insights, and deep understanding of how you came into this world, your psychological makeup, your purpose in this life, and the nature of the relationships and experiences that you will encounter along your way.

We all have our own individual horoscope, a chart that is unique to us and that is calculated from our personal data of date, place, and time of birth. Nobody else's chart can be identical to our own unless that other person is born on exactly the same day, in the same place, and at the same time. Whilst we all know our Sun sign, none of us can know our Moon sign, Mercury sign, Venus sign, and so on without consulting an Ephemerides, a book containing the planetary timetables that tell us which planet is in which sign on any given day. Furthermore, none of us can know our Ascendant—or Rising Sign—without knowing our time of birth and calculating the whole horoscope.

In the past, the craft of calculating the horoscope required the skills of a trained astrologer, but modern-day technology has changed this forever. Now the mathematical exercise of erecting a horoscope based on the exact data of an individual's date, place, and time of birth can be done online in a matter of minutes.

Simply by typing "calculating your horoscope," any search engine will direct you immediately to numerous astrology sites that offer this service. These are quick and easy to use. Entering your date, place, and time of birth will instantly produce the visual of your personal horoscope, showing you the degree and sign of your Ascendant and the exact position of all the planets on the wheel. You can find out more about the Ephemerides, your Rising Sign, and chart calculation in

Chapter Three (see p. 102). Two websites that I have found reliable in chart calculation are http://www.alwaysastrology.com/birth-chart-calculator.html and http://astrology.about.com/library/bl_freeAstrochart.htm.

If you do not know your time of birth, then simply enter 12.00 midday. This will produce what is known as a Noon Chart. Whilst this chart will not be wholly accurate in terms of the Ascendant and the position of the Moon—the swiftest moving body—you will still be able to learn the sign and degree held by the other planets. This means that you will have the necessary data for understanding the structure of your horoscope (see Chapter Four, p. 124) and also for the predictive work of transits (see Chapter Five, p. 138). Throughout this book you will find several examples of celebrities, whose birth times are not known, to illustrate how accurate this can be.

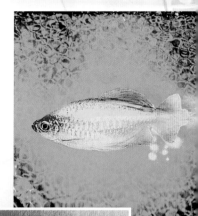

Looking at your horoscope online is sufficient for finding out which planet is in which sign for any date of birth, but for the serious student I strongly recommend drawing up the horoscope in your own hand. You need only a stack of blank wheels divided into twelve sections, which you can either make yourself or buy from any astrology shop. This will speed up your "connection" with each horoscope, as discussed further in Chapter Four.

INTERPRETING YOUR CHART

Having armed yourself with your horoscope, however, is where the value of astrological software ends. Putting it another way, this is where the worlds of astronomy and astrology divide. At an objective and mathematical level, the horoscope is generated from specific data and is firmly rooted in time and space, but at a subjective and symbolic level, the horoscope holds destiny's DNA that awaits to be unraveled and decoded.

The main focus of this book, then, is to lead the reader along the road that starts with objective information and ends with particular meaning. No software in the world can take you on that journey, as the act of interpretation—the reading of your unique astrological DNA—can be achieved only when the horoscope is aligned with context. In other words, the craft of horoscopy shows us how to marry astrological symbolism with the uniqueness of an individual's life story. Every craft needs learning and honing, and in these pages lie the tools of the astrologer's trade. Horoscopy therefore is not clairvoyance. But it is magic.

CHAPTER 1
SUN SIGNS

All astrology starts with Sun signs. At some point in your childhood you will have learned your Sun sign and, as with your own name, you almost certainly do not remember the exact moment at which you learned it. It is simply part of your identity and, somehow, even without any conscious studying, some of the key characteristics associated with your sign probably also came to be part of this unconsciously acquired knowledge.

A STARTING POINT

The horoscope shows us that we are all, in fact, a mixture of signs, but the Sun sign is nevertheless always a central consideration. The Sun symbolizes our essential self, the core of our personality and purpose around which everything else revolves. This may appear to suggest that we all can be easily pigeonholed but, as you read on, you will discover that the study of any individual horoscope reveals that this is actually very far from the truth. As to what extent you find that you are "typical" of your Sun sign is less a definitive test of astrology's accuracy than an issue that is determined by the condition of the Sun in your natal horoscope. In other words, the key characteristics of your sign will be modified to a greater or lesser extent depending on the position of the Sun in your horoscope and how it is connected to the other planets. This is further explored in Chapters Three (Houses, see p. 104) and Four (Aspects, see p. 126).

The biggest stumbling block of astrological literature is to state any kind of interpretation as if it were a given. This results only in the creation of myths rather than meaningful information, such as "all earth signs are practical," or "all fire signs are spontaneous." Such statements are obviously over-simplified and easy to dismantle. We all know earth-sign individuals who do not know one end of a screwdriver from another or fire-sign people who are not risk takers.

The following illustrations of the twelve signs of the zodiac are therefore designed to encapsulate their core meaning. The characteristics of the signs with regard to physical appearance, nature, aptitudes, and needs are based on tradition—the astrological knowledge that has been handed down to us over thousands of years—and also on my own observations and findings through client work and research that spans nearly 30 years.

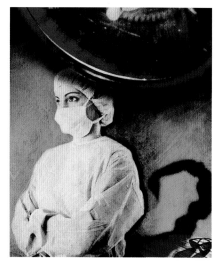

Most importantly, a sound grasp of the symbolism of the twelve signs is the bedrock of astrological interpretation and goes way beyond an understanding of just the Sun sign. As explored in the following chapter, all the planets in a horoscope have their own symbolic nature. It is the astrologer's job to unpack their particular message and meaning by interpreting how a particular planet and a particular sign work together.

Learning to think symbolically starts with the Sun signs and is crucial to the understanding of the craft of horoscopy. One of my favorite phrases when I am teaching is that "the chart is the individual, the individual is the chart." In other words, you are your chart. Astrology is not causal. No planet makes you into the kind of person that you are or dictates that you behave in a certain way. More accurately, the horoscope is a celestial mirror. Look into it, and it will reflect back to you your life, your purpose, your relationships, your vocation, your health, and so on.

The same applies to predictive astrology, looking in the mirror of the past, present, and future to see what has happened, what is happening, and what will happen, as explored in Chapter Five (see p. 138). If we say that all astrology starts with the Sun signs, we can equally say that all astrology ends with the twelve signs too. At a natal or predictive level, you will always find yourself returning to their essential symbolism, and staying true to their guidelines will keep you on track as you convert each horoscope's information into particular meaning.

ARIES

SYMBOL: THE RAM

RULING PLANET: MARS

ELEMENT AND MODE: CARDINAL FIRE

KEY PHRASE: I AM

SPOT THE ARIES

Aries rules the head and the face and you can often recognize this sign by the sharp profile, high cheekbones, an aquiline nose, and firm jaw. Look for a scar on the face, too. When you meet an Aries they tend to look you straight in the eye and ask direct and highly interested questions. They are the masters of giving undivided attention, even if they do quickly move on to the next person or the next topic of interest. Mars' color red is also a big clue. It is quite astonishing how many Aries people are red haired. You will also find that most Aries women have dyed their hair red at some point in their life, even if it does not suit them. What does suit them is a hat. Baseball caps are a favorite, but they can carry off any kind of headwear, from beach sombreros to an Ascot creation. Royal milliner Frederick Fox (April 2, 1931– December 11, 2013), who created 350 hats for the Queen and many other members of the British royal family over the span of 35 years, was an Aries.

THE ARIES NATURE

As the first sign of the zodiac, Aries people are initiators and individualists. They thrive on action and immediacy and are energetic, impatient, and direct. They are the first to volunteer to do something, and they do it straight away. They have a knack of getting straight to the point, cutting through red tape, and finding a positive answer. This is the sign of the ego, so they are also competitive and tend to regard second place as one for losers. This can be coupled with irreverence—or even total disregard for the "rules"—as they know that giving too much weight to what others might think will hold them back. Here, then, is the archetype of the pioneer and the trailblazer. Just because something has never been done before does not mean that it cannot be done now. In fact, the challenge of "finding a way" is irresistible for this can-do sign. Tucking a "first" under their belt, no matter what it may be, is possibly one of their greatest missions in life.

LOVE AND RELATIONSHIPS

It is not unusual to find that the Aries' courage often wavers when venturing into emotional territory. The fear of rejection is the fear of failure—and to feel ridiculous is an Aries nightmare. They are also speed freaks, and it is practically a knee-jerk reaction to up the tempo and race to a conclusion. In this respect, it is difficult for them to endure the courtship stage and, once partnered, they then have to learn that the "let's compromise and do it my way" approach does not work. Their

IN A NUTSHELL

immediate

incisive

direct

innovative

inspirational

effective

opposite sign of Libra—the sign of balance, partnership, and arbitration—embodies the natural skills and arts of relating that Aries has to acquire. However, their vision can often be proved right. The most successful Aries marriage I know of is of a woman who proposed after six weeks of dating with words that amounted to, "Well, are you going to marry me or what?" The couple is still together 36 years later.

Generally, for an Aries to be happy in love, there must never be any risk of playing second fiddle. Love triangles are a no-no, as are long-distance relationships. The need to feel special and prized is an essential ingredient in the Aries life and, in their love life, it is indispensable.

VOCATION

Fiercely independent, those born under this Mars sign are not ideally suited for teamwork, unless they happen to be team leader, of course. They are generally self-starters and are capable of phenomenal single-mindedness. They are "project people" and therefore unlikely to stay in the same job for years on end. In the words of an Aries client, "We like to set it up, put in a plan, ensure it's working, then we're bored and ready to move on."

Whatever their chosen profession, the Aries goal is not just to achieve but to excel, and at some point in the conversation they usually manage to tell you how good they are at their job. They are absolutely brilliant at self-advertisement, they believe in hard work and striving for what they want and have little time for the moaners and complainers of this world.

The flip side of the Aries coin is the "self"-ish streak and a capacity for diva behavior. But when they are fired up with a worthwhile cause—then it is a completely different story. Suddenly the tables are turned and they are selfless in the role of inspirer or role model. As natural defenders, they will move mountains in order to help someone in genuine need. Many Aries people are to be found in the caring professions that require fight as opposed to pity, such as social work or human rights. They are natural born crusaders and delight in making a difference.

HEALTH

A typical Aries does not need any instructions when it comes to living it up, but all fire signs have to be careful of "burnout." It is too easy for this sign to overdo things, to burn the candle at both ends, and they have to learn to slow down occasionally and recharge their batteries. Early warning signs of depletion are afflictions such as headaches, migraines, or sinusitis. They are also prone to all Mars' heat-related conditions, such as burns, fevers, rashes and inflammation, bites or stings, injuries incurred through haste, such as cuts or grazes, sports injuries, or strains to the body incurred when not recognizing their physical limitations.

TAURUS

(APRIL 21–MAY 21)

SYMBOL: THE BULL
RULING PLANET: VENUS
ELEMENT AND MODE: FIXED EARTH
KEY PHRASE: I POSSESS

SPOT THE TAURUS

Taurus rules the neck. You will occasionally come across the long swan variety, but more usually Taureans are distinguishable by the short, muscular "bull" neck atop broad shoulders. Their faces bear an uncanny resemblance to cows, in the nicest possible sense. Look for the bovine square face, the gentle eyes, the placid expression, and that thoughtful look that they adopt as they chew the cud. The men tend to be typically masculine with strong solid bodies, barrel-chested, and with pronounced square chins. The women can be either stocky or tall but are usually exceptionally feminine—look for the ribbons and bows. When untroubled, both sexes ooze serenity, softness, and sensuality. You will occasionally come across a skinny, wiry Taurean, but more usually they tend to have slow metabolisms, they love their food and battle with their weight. Taurus also rules the throat, so listen for the slow, rich, resonant, earthy, or gravelly voice.

THE TAURUS NATURE

The typical Taurus nature is steady and unhurried. Patient, kind, and good-natured, their approach is slow, deliberate, and they tend to be risk averse. They are usually at their best when able to do things in their own way and in their own time, or if arrangements are made with plenty of advance warning. On a bad day, they are slow to the point of inertia, lazy, or just plain obstinate. If you try to rush them, they will dig their heels in even deeper. When goaded, which usually takes extreme provocation, you will see the steely glint in the eye or witness the raging bull in full explosion. Clear a half-mile radius and leave them well alone for up to three days.

When dealing with a crisis, however, this sign has a reputation for staying serene under pressure. They generally will not get steamed up about their own issues or on anyone else's behalf. They have huge reserves of common sense and will click into sensible mode and deal with matters in a hands-on way. Tolerance and droll humor are their saving graces, and they can be hilariously funny.

LOVE AND RELATIONSHIPS

With their own brand of earthy charm and humor, Taureans can be incredibly sociable and entertaining. This, however, sometimes gives the wrong impression in the dating game. Their dislike of being pushed or pressured definitely extends to their love life. Their sensual appetite means that they are perfectly capable of having flings like everyone else, but they are probably the least likely sign to enter into a

IN A NUTSHELL

stoical

reliable

sensuous

appetitive

tolerant

risk averse

committed relationship in haste. Their top must-have is safety, and the slightest hint of insincerity or behavior that makes them feel uncomfortable is enough to prompt a huge step back.

Once in love, Taureans make for rock-solid and loyal partners. They tend to live and let live rather than find fault, they have a long fuse, and they value the relaxation, loving sex, and companionship of genuine attachment. The flip side of the coin is that they can endure discontent for a long time and, just as they are slow to commit, they are also slow to leave. This earth sign finds it hard to climb out of ruts, often preferring familiarity, financial security, and their creature comforts to the lure of new adventures.

VOCATION

With their innate persistence and pragmatic streak, Taureans can turn their hands to pretty much anything when it comes to bringing home the bacon. Being connoisseurs of comfort, security, and retail therapy, they dislike constantly having to make ends meet. They would rather slog away at something menial than be broke, but there is always the danger of creating and staying in that legendary Taurus rut as a result.

Together, the sign of Taurus and ruling planet Venus govern money, produce, women, and beauty. Job satisfaction is, ultimately, important for this sign and is often discovered through a connection with nature. Taureans do not mind getting their hands dirty, and here we find them in the farming and food industries, from the land workers who grow the crops to the chef who serves up gourmet meals. Pottery and floristry are also part of the picture of working with the earth and producing objects of art and beauty. Many Taureans have a keen interest in fashion, too, and are talented artists with a sensual feel for fabrics and designs. The financial sectors, such as banking and accountancy, are also traditional Taurus roles.

With the Taurus rulership of the throat, many Taureans are drawn to the music industry. In particular, this sign tends to produce distinctive singers, as exemplified by Barbara Streisand (b. April 24, 1942), Willie Nelson (b. April 29, 1933), Joe Cocker (b. May 20, 1944), Roy Orbison (b. 23 April, 1936) and Adele (b. May 5, 1988), to name but a few.

HEALTH

Those born under the sign of the Bull tend to be hardy creatures, often blessed with a strong, stocky physique. They usually enjoy robust health and seem to escape the endless list of minor ailments to which others are prone. Their stamina levels tend to be higher than average, or they are simply good at pacing themselves. What may come across as laziness is often a type of built-in physical regulator, allowing them to meet the physical demands on their body by expending the minimum amount of energy required.

When their immune system does let them down, it comes as no surprise to learn that this sign is susceptible to sore throats, tonsillitis, laryngitis, swollen glands, or problems related to the vocal chords or thyroid. This sign also rules the gums and the middle ear. Weight is the other issue. As the sign of the senses, they are often comfort eaters and can pile on the pounds at a rate of knots.

Textbook
TAUREANS

Pop and country singer **Kelly Clarkson** (b. April 24, 1982) who, with her powerful, growly voice sang her way to victory in the first American Idol, and whose continually fluctuating weight became a subject of obsessive media scrutiny.

Jay Leno (b. April 28, 1950), comedian and television host whose autobiography is called *Leading with my Chin*. He has donated thousands to charity Feminist Majority, to help the plight of women in Afghanistan.

Donatella Versace (b. May 2, 1955), vice president and chief designer at Versace, she took the helm to continue and promote brother Gianni Versace's legacy and empire after his untimely death.

II GEMINI

SYMBOL: THE TWINS
RULING PLANET: MERCURY
ELEMENT AND MODE: MUTABLE AIR
KEY PHRASE: I SPEAK

SPOT THE GEMINI

Gemini rules the lungs, nervous system, shoulders, arms, and hands. You can often spot this excitable sign by the way they gesticulate in order to express themselves. As the communicators of the zodiac, talking is as natural as breathing, but if you asked them to sit on their hands, most Geminis would be rendered mute. They are rarely overweight, as they run off nervous energy and tend to under-eat or burn calories at a rate of knots. They find it hard to be still, but this chirpy sign in full flow is your original breath of fresh air, cracking jokes, laughing easily, and chattering away to anyone about anything. There is something bird-like in their quick, restless movements and bright, inquisitive eyes that reflect a busy brain, ceaselessly computing information. Youthfulness is a hallmark of this sign and often shows in their dress sense, too. Look for checks, stripes, or a riot of contrasting colors and styles.

THE GEMINI NATURE

Gemini's archetype is the *Puer aeternus/Puella aeterna*, the eternal youth. In physical terms, they tend to look younger than their years, naturally or through artifice, but very often it is the former. Their approach is light and playful, sometimes irreverent, as they refuse to take life or authority too seriously. Their sense of fun shows in a quick wit, a slapstick sense of humor, and a childlike enthusiasm for games, ideas, and suggestions. A typical Gemini is up for anything if it promises to be a laugh. They thrive on company and conversation, and, with their butterfly minds, they can flit from subject to subject, rarely lost for words.

The sign of the Twins has a Jekyll and Hyde reputation that is unjustified and misleading. Just because they can be changeable does not mean that they have a split personality—think multifaceted rather than two-faced—and look for the "doubling up" twin symbolism, such as two jobs, two cars, two dogs, two marriages, and an inability to buy or own just one of anything.

LOVE AND RELATIONSHIPS

Geminis may at first be attracted to the person who listens to them, but having someone hang on their every word is not their idea of a relationship. Love talk, or any kind of talk, for a Gemini is most definitely a dialogue not a monologue. This sign needs a meeting of minds, someone to play verbal volleyball with, someone who challenges them, makes them think and laugh, someone who will work and play with them, but who will always hold their attention and understand their complexities.

II
IN A NUTSHELL

multitasking

animated

talkative

inventive

resourceful

mischievous

Commitment is not always easy for a Gemini as they are such free spirits. The moment that they sense any danger of being cornered, they simply slide away, so a long string of affairs until they meet "the one" is not unusual. However, it is also in their nature to "go along" with things, so the other typical scenario is to make an early first marriage that they then quickly grow out of, unless the relationship itself is one that evolves with them. Usually, a second, later marriage is more successful. They are secretly sentimental under that sometimes-glib exterior and can blossom with the emotional stability of the right partner.

VOCATION

Ruled by Mercury, the winged messenger of the gods, Gemini rules everything connected to the communication industry. Anything media-related—marketing, journalism and reporting, television or radio broadcasting and presenting—Geminis are naturals when it comes to spreading the news, they think incredibly fast on their feet and are talented at using the written or spoken word. This sign also rules driving and professions such as bus or cab drivers.

Geminis are often called the "jack-of-all-trades and master of none," which, up to a point, is true. This does not mean that they are incapable of excelling in their chosen career, but that they can be bored easily and need the mental stimulus of variety. They are natural multi-taskers, automatically doing more than one thing at a time, mentally and physically. Their hands can be busy with one job while their brain is engaged with something entirely different. They can solve a work problem, write a shopping list, eat their lunch, and plan a family event simultaneously.

As the Peter Pan of the zodiac, there is also something elusive about this sign and the buck never stops on the Gemini desk if they can possibly help it. A Gemini client insists that he made it to marketing director not through talent or any particular focus, but by "ducking and diving" his way up the career ladder. The duplicity of this sign knows that language conceals as well as reveals, they are clever and crafty, for good or ill, and can talk their way out of any corner.

HEALTH

Unsurprisingly, Geminis need their downtime. While their mental energy is legendary, this can tip over into hyperactivity, and they do not always notice when their physical energy is running out. They habitually take on far too much and are consequently prone to nervous exhaustion. More haste, less speed is part of this picture. When they fail to pace themselves properly, they will be slowed down through accidents or falls that produce broken bones, strains, or injuries mostly to the hands, arms, or shoulders. This sign, along with Mercury, also rules the respiratory system and all conditions or problems related to the chest and lungs.

CANCER

SYMBOL: THE CRAB

RULING PLANET: THE MOON

ELEMENT AND MODE: CARDINAL WATER

KEY PHRASE: I SECURE

SPOT THE CANCER

The only sign ruled by the Moon, the typical Cancerian face tends towards roundness. Many men, in particular, born under this sign have the classic "Man in the Moon" look, complete with picture-book dimples and a wide smile. In women, even when the other features are long or sharp, there is often still a fullness in the cheeks that creates the circular look. The eyes are luminous with flecks of other colors, including the silvery glint of moonlight, and they telegraph care and sympathy. However, the popular image of Cancerians as shy and retiring wallflowers is far from the truth. While they may be cautious initially, they have a wicked sense of clownish fun. Cancer rules the stomach, so watch for the smile breaking into a real belly laugh that is unbelievably infectious. As with the image of the waning and waxing moon, there is something malleable about their features, and they are natural mimics, too.

THE CANCERIAN NATURE

As the sign of the Crab, a Cancerian's knee-jerk response is evasion, to crab-walk sideways rather than confront head on. In their daily interactions, they tend to take the scenic route, sometimes going all around the houses before finally getting to the point. This springs from their own sensitivity, the fear of offending or wounding, as they themselves can find challenging types abrasive or intimidating. The dislike of directness is part of their charm and diplomacy but can also tip over into uncertainty, second-guessing, going off at tangents, or protracted going around in circles.

The constantly changing face of the moon also reflects the multifaceted Cancer nature. On a good day, they are funny, sweet, and affectionate, drawing others towards them like a magnet and letting everyone know how much they are liked and cared for. On a bad day, they can be downright crabby, withdrawn—into the famous shell—or needy. Those crab claws can also cling to grievances and brood over old hurts. One of the Cancer lessons is to learn how to unhook and let go.

LOVE AND RELATIONSHIPS

The Moon rules our emotional nature, needs, and home life, thus Cancerians are especially known for their attachment to family. For good or ill, there is usually an incredibly strong tie to at least one of the parents. They are protective of their loved ones, but the nurturing instinct often reaches beyond blood ties. Rather than collect

IN A NUTSHELL

indirect

cautious

evasive

sympathetic

instinctive

tenacious

a wide circle of acquaintances, it is in the Cancer nature to "adopt" their chosen few, creating an extended family. Nobody can storm the barricades, but once someone is accepted into that inner sanctum, they are usually there for life.

The crab shell hides an extremely soft center that is secretly, or not so secretly, romantic and sentimental. When in love, Cancerians make for committed and loyal partners but need absolute trust and emotional security in order to thrive. Their high levels of receptivity are signs of finely tuned instincts, but, if they feel abandoned or misunderstood, they can be touchy and desperately unhappy. They are not always the most articulate of signs. As one Cancer client says, "I find it difficult to explain, to put things into words, but I can sense the slightest of emotions." A partner who understands this is a top must-have.

VOCATION

Cancerians are compassionate and tend to be natural carers and rescuers. When they are tuned into the world, these individuals can do a lot of good and are frequently found in charity work or the caring professions, such as nursing or looking after the elderly. Jobs related to children also belong to this sign, everything from running a nursery or play group, right through to nannies or foster parenting, regardless of whether they personally have the maternal or paternal urge to have their own children.

Cancerians are also surprisingly good business people, so do not be fooled by the "home and hearth" reputation. They may be cautious, but they are also shrewd, brilliant at maneuvering, and their persistence is second to none. Tenacity is a hallmark of the entrepreneurial type, underlying the total dedication to a cause and the refusal to give up easily. For a Cancerian, this is enriched by a desire to create security for their dependents or to act in some way as a spokesperson for their generation. At some instinctive level, they understand that they are passing on the baton.

HEALTH

As this sign rules the stomach, Cancerians tend to move from their "gut" reactions. This is where they physically register their feelings and responses, to the extent of feeling "sick to the stomach" when wounded by others. Food allergies, acid stomach, IBS, or water retention are common afflictions.

Possibly more than any other sign, there is a powerful link between the emotional and the physical. This sign also rules the breast and the uterus, and if there was a lack or total absence of nurturing and mirroring in the early years, this can leave a very deep wound that is hard to heal. In extreme cases, there is a tendency to internalize pain, resulting in the expression of psychological conflict through somatic symptoms.

The sanctuary of home is tantamount to that of a health farm. Most Cancerians are natural homemakers, whether it be in a mansion or bedsit, and relaxation in their own space is crucial to their wellbeing.

Textbook
CANCERIANS

Nelson Mandela (July 18, 1918–December 5, 2013), aka Tata (father) and described as "the father of the nation" of South Africa, whose legendary quotes include "There can be no keener revelation of a society's soul than the way in which it treats its children."

Diana, Princess of Wales (July 1, 1961–August 31, 1997), the original yummy mummy, whose tireless and compassionate charity work earned her the accolade of "the people's princess." Her son, and fellow Cancerian, Prince William, Duke of Cambridge (b. June 21, 1982), continues her legacy.

Meryl Streep (b. June 22, 1949), a legend in her lifetime and applauded in particular for her unparalleled ability to imitate accents. Also known for a rock-solid home life, four children, and quoted as saying she was "wired for family."

LEO

SYMBOL: THE LION
RULING PLANET: THE SUN
ELEMENT AND MODE: FIXED FIRE
KEY PHRASE: I CREATE

IN A NUTSHELL

creative

proud

warm

self reliant

efficient

assured

SPOT THE LEO

You only have to think of a full-grown lion to get the Leo picture. Regal, proud, sometimes imposing or magnificent, sometimes just plain cuddly, these individuals are hard to miss, not that they would let you. This sign commands attention, and Leos have a way of announcing themselves. While everyone else may just walk into a room, a typical Leo, consciously or not, makes an entrance and turns heads. Leo rules the back, and you can often spot this sign by their straight spines and excellent posture. Look out, too, for the graceful feline movements, the big cat profile, the broad face, Roman nose, and the mane. Many Leos have long, thick, or shaggy hair, and the women generally prefer to be blonde or to "big up" their tresses with highlights. Also look for sun-kissed faces, bright clothing, and statement jewelry.

THE LEO NATURE

As the only sign ruled by the Sun, Leo individuals are to be found at the center of their own universes. They have a knack for being at the heart of things, the one around whom all others revolve, and they make wonderful hosts. The Sun rules the monarchy, pomp, and circumstance, and Leos are the kings and queens of the zodiac. They thrive on "strokes," which they will court, either blatantly or subtly, and they gravitate towards the warmth of good feeling and bask in the rays. Here is the image of the big cat, luxuriating, yawning, and purring, at nobody's beck and call but its own. Some Leos do have a tendency to indolence in this respect, but usually in a contented, relaxed, "don't bother me" way.

Leo also rules the heart, and this sign is hearty and expansive. You do get the small cat introverts, but, more typically, a Leo is the one holding center stage, lapping up attention and compliments. They also revel in drama and can easily create one when life gets too tame, but all they really want is to be adored.

LOVE AND RELATIONSHIPS

Leos are often the backbone of their family. They secretly like to think that everything would fall apart if they were not there holding it all together and, up to a point, they are probably right. They do, however, need to guard against arrogance, bossiness, or interference. They have to learn to bite their lip or look the other way when their fingers itch to take over a job, especially when preserving family relationships and equilibrium.

To be happy in love, their golden rule is never to settle for half measures. Playing the hated second fiddle is never a workable option. The ideal Leo partner is someone who wants to make them the center of their world, someone who makes no secret of their adoration, who is their number one fan, fiercely loyal and lavish with their praise, time, love—and money. Meanness is a Leo's biggest no-no. They need a mate who takes genuine pleasure in spoiling them and boosting their confidence.

Big hearted, warm, and generous, they will naturally attract a gathering, but genuine friendships are more hard won. They place enormous value on their personal dignity and find it hard to let the mask slip. Ask them how they are and nine times out of ten they will answer anything from "fine" to "fabulous," no matter what ordeal or hardships they may be going through.

VOCATION

Lions are at their best when they are "Top Cat" and ideally need to be self employed, the boss, or in a position of responsibility. They are natural-born organizers and have their biggest chance of success in any managerial or promotional role that allows bold self-expression and creativity. They love to stamp any enterprise with their own individual hallmark, and straitjackets of any kind are a death-knell. This sign rules jobs connected to the stage, amusements, and gambling and produces many mesmerizing entertainers and performers.

True, they may have a tendency to take over at the drop of a hat, but such is the nature of their entrepreneurial spirit. They have vision as well as creativity, they can see how something needs to be done, and they take a fierce pride in whatever stirs their dedication. However, this is nearly always as much for personal satisfaction as for public acclaim. In the process, the Leo lesson is to allow space for other people's needs, opinions, and egos, as embodied in the opposite sign of Aquarius, sign of the group and objectivity. Leos may learn the hard way that pride goes before a fall, but they have the courage to dust themselves off and start all over again.

HEALTH

Both the Sun and Leo rule the heart and the back, the two major "life supports" of the body. Many Leos will suffer from a back problem of some kind in the course of their lives, especially when they feel unsupported, unneeded, or unappreciated. This can lead to inertia, depression, or illness, and there is nothing sadder than an unloved, lonely Leo. More than any other sign, Leos thrive and survive on unconditional regard and wither without it. A broken heart or a healthy heart, so much depends on their ability to find personal happiness and contentment. Cholesterol levels are also especially important for this sign.

VIRGO

SYMBOL: THE VIRGIN
RULING PLANET: MERCURY
ELEMENT AND MODE: MUTABLE EARTH
KEY PHRASE: I SERVE

SPOT THE VIRGO

Virgos have a reputation for perfectionism, and this often shows in their physical appearance. Designer labels or off the peg, look for the individual who is immaculately put together and who is a triumph of cleanliness and perfect grooming. A typical Virgo would not dream of leaving the house in a hurry, wearing anything stained or in need of repair. The men tend to have square, rugged, yet slightly boyish faces and can be noticeably dapper. The women tend to go to the extremes of immaculate makeup and accessories or the fresh, barefaced look that simply radiates good health. Even if there is scant attention to fashion or adornment, there is a distinct neatness, crispness, or minimalism to the Virgo look. Everything may be slightly understated but do not be fooled. It can take ages to look this good. Virgos are also the worriers of the zodiac, so look for the pensive expression or the frown.

THE VIRGO NATURE

Many people naturally associate Mercury, planet of language and the mind, with his better-known masculine sign, communicative, live-wire Gemini. Virgo is Mercury's feminine sign, which is expressed through brainpower of a more subtle and exacting kind. Virgo's primary task is to evaluate and analyze. Information, feelings, and decisions are all fed through some kind of mental sieve, separating fact from fiction and isolating essential details. If they ask you a question, which they generally love to do, they will pick apart your answer to find out exactly and precisely what you mean.

This sign is not given to extravagance or lavishness. Virgo is economical with all resources and can be frugal to the point of extreme self-denial. They can be fanatically tidy and fussy, with a place for everything and everything in its place. However, the goody-two-shoes image is frequently a cover for inner turmoil and a wonderfully whacky streak, which most certainly does not tally with the somewhat dry and boring image often ascribed to this sign.

LOVE AND RELATIONSHIPS

There are probably more myths to debunk with this sign than any other. All Virgos are prim and prudish, right? Wrong. In public they may come across as demure, but behind closed doors they are perfectly capable of raunchiness. This is an earth sign after all. Are they really critical fusspots? It is true that an insecure Virgo excels at nagging and nit-picking, but usually they would be the first to admit it. Their line of defense is along the lines of wanting the best out of their relationship, wanting their

IN A NUTSHELL

fastidious

analytical

diligent

dutiful

quirky

astute

partner to be the best that they can be, and wanting to feel safe so that they can relax. Note that this generally does not work the other way around. Virgos are positively allergic to criticism. They will bristle with indignation and feel wounded to the quick. They have a lot invested in their hard-working, perfection-seeking approach and beliefs.

A Virgo's saving grace is that their highest standards are almost certainly their own and a partner who understands just how hard Virgos can be on themselves is a must-have. A partner who pulls their weight is also crucial. Virgos, in return, need to feel respect and low achievers or idle dreamers need not apply.

VOCATION

Virgos have a dutiful streak a mile wide and this sign is aligned to service, everything from the armed forces serving their country to trades people serving the general public. This is also the sign of skills and crafts, reflecting the Virgo's unparalleled talent for precision and keen eye for detail. They adopt the policy that, if something is worth doing, then it is worth doing faultlessly or not at all. They have self-discipline, a strong work ethic, and can easily become workaholics, especially as they find it pretty much impossible to delegate. Whom else could they trust to do a task to their own staggeringly high standards? Other people's inefficiency or slapdash attitude can drive them nuts, but they do have to learn when "good enough" is acceptable rather than continually striving for perfection. However, job satisfaction lies in continually honing their expertise and in approaching every task with patience and painstaking exactitude. This often springs from being afraid to make mistakes, which, as a result, are rare and never repeated.

Thorough and systematic, this sign rules administrative work of all kinds, but a Virgo will excel in any job that demands accuracy. They can also express their mental agility through the written word and often make excellent writers and public speakers. This sign rules health, too, so many Virgos are drawn to the medical professions, from nursing through to speech or occupational therapy and often specializing in a particular field.

HEALTH

Part of the Virgo bad press is the tag of hypochondria. More accurately, Virgos are generally health conscious to the extreme, if only because their most common ailment is anxiety. They worry about their health, just as they tend to worry about all sorts of things. They can worry for the world. They can worry about not having anything to worry about. At their most fretful, Virgos become cranky, withdrawn, or ill. In the physical body Virgo rules the pancreas and intestines, so fear, stress, or imbalances are most likely to manifest in intestinal or assimilation problems for this sign. They are prone to food allergies and are usually suited to a diet specifically tailored to their sensitive system.

LIBRA

SYMBOL: THE SCALES
RULING PLANET: VENUS
ELEMENT AND MODE: CARDINAL AIR
KEY PHRASE: I RELATE

SPOT THE LIBRA

Venus' first sign is Taurus, who embodies the earthy sensual nature of this planet, her second is Libra, the sign of the Scales. The obvious themes of balance and symmetry often show in the physical appearance and, as Venus rules beauty itself, many Librans are real good lookers. The chief characteristics are well-proportioned faces, regular features, a full sensual mouth, a seductive smile, and sometimes dimples in the cheeks or the chin. The eyes are usually large, almond shaped, and beautiful, whatever the color. Librans are natural socialites, but they tend not to play to the gallery and can find the role of social butterfly tiring or superficial. You are more likely to find them engaged in earnest, one to one conversations. Librans also have an eye for fashion and can pick out the right outfit at twenty paces. Casual or dressed up to the nines, the look is stylish and perfectly coordinated.

THE LIBRA NATURE

The constant weighing of the scales, listing the pros and cons, considering all angles, and the desire to arrive at a balanced judgment all lie at the root of Libra's reputation for dithering and indecision. When you have a conversation that is peppered with "on the other hand," "all things considered," "to be fair," and "what do you think?" you will know you are talking to a Libra. As with all the air signs, they love to chat, but they especially love to bounce their thoughts and ideas off others and collect different views and opinions.

The famous Scales also symbolize the two sides to a partnership, and most Librans are natural diplomats. They have huge amounts of charm, and their powers of negotiation, arbitration, and compromise are second to none. On a good day, they are sweetness and light personified. However, when ruffled, tired, or unfulfilled, Librans suffer from a lack of purpose or sense of urgency and can be seriously cranky, argumentative, and chaotic. Their opposite sign of Aries embodies the directness and immediacy that Libra struggles to acquire.

LOVE AND RELATIONSHIPS

Relationships are of course important for everyone, but for a Libran they amount to life support. A one-sided set of scales is of no use, to anyone, so Librans are wired for partnership and generally dislike doing things solo. Loneliness can be their biggest fear, sometimes to the extent of spending time with people whom they do not especially like. Conversely, they may find themselves saddled with difficult people

IN A NUTSHELL

sociable

charming

indecisive

diplomatic

discursive

fair

because they find it so hard to say no and dread giving offence. It takes a lot for a Libra to reject. They are the ultimate people pleasers or rescuers and easily fall into the trap of trying to be everything to everyone. However, they have a shy streak and often find it hard to ask for what they want in return.

Unsurprisingly, it is rare for a Libran to be without a relationship for any great length of time. The next partner seems to materialize with surprising ease, much to the chagrin of their single friends. They make it look very easy. The flip side of the coin is the "someone is better than no-one" trap, over-dependency or neediness, but ultimately they value mental chemistry. Of all the signs, they are the most likely to make a success of a platonic relationship, especially if there is a meeting of minds and enjoyable companionship.

VOCATION

As one of the Venus-ruled signs, many Librans are found in the beauty industry and professions that relate to makeup, perfume, lotions, and potions. Anything that makes you feel good and look good is the Libra domain, so here we also find the fashion designers and jewelry experts of the zodiac. If you want to de-junk and revamp your wardrobe, enlist a Libran. Apart from the fact that they love to be needed and take pleasure in helping you, they have a natural feel for style and fabrics. This is where their indecisive streak disappears. They have very definite tastes, they know what suits them—and you—and they can put the perfect outfit together in a matter of minutes. This talent also extends to interior design, and a typical Libra home will be a place of great beauty, comfort, and luxury. A bed is not a bed unless it is piled high with cushions; a living room is not a living room unless it is rich with soft furnishings and *objets d'art*.

Libra's sociable nature and ability to charm, smooth, and soothe can also lead to great success in the diplomatic and business worlds. In addition to a definite taste for the high life, they excel at wining, dining, and PR. The fair-minded nature of this sign also lends them to legal careers, such as judges, magistrates, and any work in a court of law.

HEALTH

Libra rules the kidneys. With their love of good living, Librans need to flush out the old and keep their lives moving. Illnesses may arise from over-indulgence or inactivity, or the inertia of depression. They invariably have a sweet tooth and need to control their sugar intake to ward off the risk of diabetes. They tend to have extremely sensitive blood sugar levels and their energy can plummet without regular fuel.

Find me a Libran who does not love a bath. This is where they soak away the tensions of each day and quiet the noise in their busy heads. Here they find solitude rather than the dreaded loneliness, the oasis in their constantly interactive world. Librans have to learn firm boundaries to protect themselves from other people's stress and not feel guilty about it.

SCORPIO

SYMBOL: THE SCORPION
RULING PLANET: MARS CO-RULER: PLUTO
ELEMENT AND MODE: FIXED WATER
KEY PHRASE: I REGENERATE

SPOT THE SCORPIO

Scorpios exude powerful charisma, but this goes hand in hand with being mysterious and secretive. As the sign of fixed water, they are either the "still waters run deep" type, bewitching but unfathomable, with dark brown or nearly black eyes, or they present the frozen, glacial front, often with startling light or ice-blue eyes. Many Scorpio women, in particular, have that "ice-maiden" type of beauty. Both types and both sexes are expert at the poker face that gives absolutely nothing away. In the rare moments that you catch them off guard, or without their beloved sunglasses, you will notice that the Scorpio eyes are piercing and mesmerizing, even hypnotic. Many exude a sultry sexuality and favor the color black. In social situations they tend not to take the lead, preferring to observe and test the water first. First impressions are of someone restrained, thoughtful, private, and unreadable.

THE SCORPIO NATURE

There is nothing meek and mild about this sign. Even if they come across as easygoing or flippant, do not be fooled. Emotional intensity is the hallmark of the Scorpio nature, and they rarely register indifference, to anything or anyone. You can often sense hidden depths and an iron will behind the mask, and when they fix you with that intense, probing gaze, you have good reason to feel slightly uncomfortable. Very little escapes their notice, and if you feel as if your every word is being analyzed—it is because it is. A Scorpio loves nothing better than to find out what makes you tick, but at first it's a one-way street. It takes time to get to know a Scorpio to the extent of being allowed into their private world in return.

What about that famous scorpion's sting in the tail? There is a vengeful side to this sign, but it is usually saved for when their jealousy is inflamed or when they feel deeply wounded or wronged. The whole gamut of feelings, from love to hate, runs deep, and they can be fiercely loyal or unforgiving with equal purple passion.

LOVE AND RELATIONSHIPS

Scorpios tend to have a higher than average libido. Scorpio rules the whole life and death cycle, hence the connection to regeneration and procreation, and in the search for a mate they are not beneath exploiting their sex appeal to the full. Male Scorpios have a highly charged sexual magnetism, and many of the women are classic "femme fatale." Think Vivien Leigh (b. November 5, 1913) in *Gone with the Wind*. As one documentary described her, "She taught us how to flirt."

IN A NUTSHELL

determined

forceful

thorough

intense

passionate

resourceful

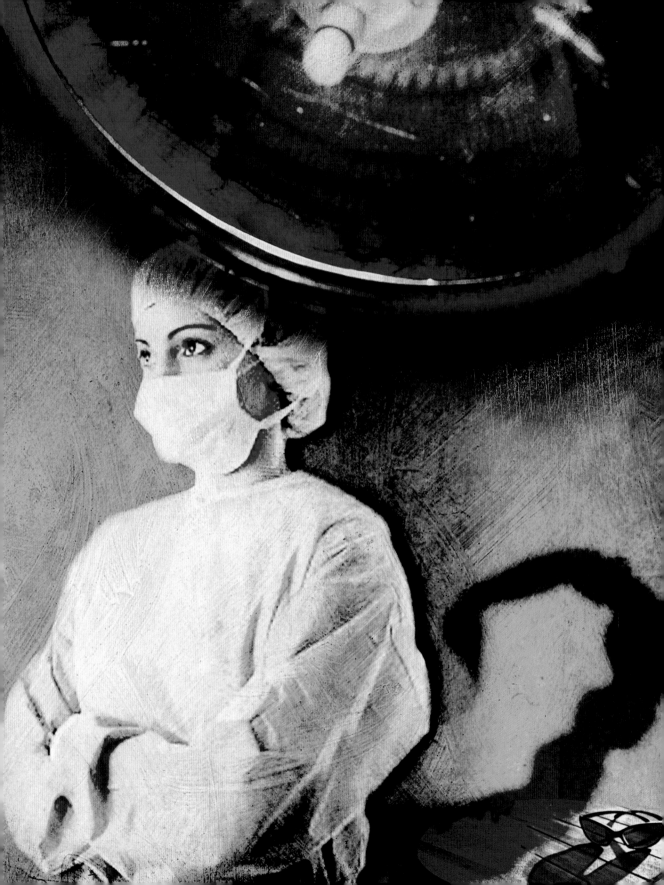

Scorpios take everything seriously and their love life is no exception. Generally, there are no half measures. They may be capable of strings of affairs but, when it comes to genuine commitment, they are the least likely sign to settle for anything less than the real deal. The same applies to friendships, and they are more likely to have a few select and very close soul mates than a wide circle of superficial acquaintances. They would rather stay single than get hitched to someone they cannot love with mind, body, and soul. This is fortuitous as the wrong relationship for Scorpios can be the source of utter misery. Conversely, any kind of unhappiness or rejection can trigger their own capability of becoming destructive, controlling or cruel.

VOCATION

Traditionally ruled by Mars, planet of action and war, this sign is forceful, determined, and extremely persistent. Power and control are central issues for Scorpios, and they get a massive kick out of achievement, especially of the "against all odds" variety. Tell them that something cannot be done and they will be the first to set out to prove that it can. This may sound supremely competitive, but in truth Scorpios are often more in competition with themselves than with anyone else.

Scorpios are at their best when doing a job they feel passionate about, but they also need a long leash. They do not thrive when constrained by rules and regulations, particularly those that are designed to keep them in the position of humble employee. Scorpios do not do subservience. They would rather be broke.

Scorpio's redemption is to be found in the nature of their co-ruler, Pluto, commonly referred to as the planet of transformation, which is also captured in the symbol of the phoenix. In real terms, Scorpios embody this death and rebirth imagery through their endurance and survival skills. It is not uncommon for a Scorpio to end one way of life, to walk away and start again, often totally from scratch and often more than once. They are not unduly attached to the material world, although they are quite capable of amassing wealth, if only because money is power.

As god of the underworld, Pluto also links Scorpio to the realms of the unconscious and death. Depth psychology, psychoanalysis, detective work, healing, and psychic practices all belong to this sign, as does the work of surgeons, forensic scientists, hospice workers, bereavement counselors, and undertakers.

HEALTH

Scorpio rules elimination and all bodily outlets, the reproductive system and sexual organs, and all illnesses or afflictions associated with these parts of the body. Promiscuity is problematic, because of their susceptibility to sexually transmitted diseases, and the emotional vulnerability that they hide so well. Women often struggle with problems related to menstruation, fertility, and menopause.

Stress management is important too. They are prone to taking the kind of risks most people would avoid and do not suffer fools gladly. Scorpios have to learn and acquire the "live and let live" tolerance of their opposite sign, safety-loving Taurus.

SAGITTARIUS (NOVEMBER 23–DECEMBER 22)

SYMBOL: THE ARCHER
RULING PLANET: JUPITER
ELEMENT AND MODE: MUTABLE FIRE
KEY PHRASE: I SEEK

SPOT THE SAGITTARIUS

Jupiter is Mr. Big of the skies, and it is unusual to find a small Sagittarian. They are either tall, big boned, or larger than life. However, even the smaller versions usually give the impression of boundless energy and are often in a tearing hurry. Sagittarius rules the hips and thighs, so look for that long swinging stride or even the gallop. They may remind you of a racehorse, or of a rather large exuberant dog when they bump into you, step on your feet, or knock over your drink. Look for the big smile and the narrow, usually deep-set, quizzical eyes that meet your gaze with a disarming frankness. A quiet Sagittarian is a rarity, as most of them are party animals who thrive on the stimulus of company and conversation. Listen for the loud voice, ringing laughter, and direct questions. This can come across as rudeness, but Sagittarians tend to wear their hearts on their sleeves and forget that not everyone else does.

THE SAGITTARIAN NATURE

All the fire signs exude an obvious and immediate warmth, but Sagittarians are especially welcoming and cheerful. Friendliness is their hallmark, they expect to be liked, and they are puzzled or hurt when they are not. They can put even the most uncomfortable person at ease. Unfortunately, they can also unwittingly create discomfort when their arrows of truths hit the mark with a stinging accuracy that can leave their target speechless. They usually dig themselves into an even deeper hole when trying to explain or apologize.

However, there is no malice aforethought. They speak as they find, and they can dish out compliments with the same outspokenness. Their language is emphatic and peppered with words such as absolutely and totally. They have an infectious sense of fun and can be hilariously funny, either in a clownish way or through wit.

A typical Sagittarius is honest, gregarious, and generous. Never ask them to buy anything for you without being very specific. The idea of less is more is alien to them and you can easily end up with enough goodies to lay in for a siege.

LOVE AND RELATIONSHIPS

Sagittarians place enormous value on freedom and personal space. Marrying too early, unless it is to a real kindred spirit, can be disastrous, as they invariably end up feeling trapped or restricted. Ideally, this sign needs to sow more than the average number of wild oats and, in this respect, it is not unusual for these freewheeling individuals to go through a long period of promiscuity—and broken hearts on both

IN A NUTSHELL

intuitive

spontaneous

optimistic

friendly

enthusiastic

ethical

sides—before finding the right partner. When they are ready to commit, they do it optimistically, enthusiastically, and with total loyalty. Even so, the best partnerships often have a flavor of the unconventional, as any kind of claustrophobia is a death-knell to their emotional growth and intellectual needs. They will always respect a partner's right to individuality and independence, and they are the most likely sign to make a success of a long-distance relationship, or a match with someone from a different culture.

Family may be scattered far and wide, but real closeness tends to be confined to just one or two special relatives. Friendship, on the other hand, is hugely important to this sign, and typically they have a huge circle of people in whom they invest a great deal of love and energy. An easily jealous partner would therefore last about five minutes, and a true Sagittarian would always choose the single life over the shackles of a controlling relationship.

VOCATION

The love of personal liberty can sometimes lead to a somewhat nomadic life and a resistance to taking on responsibilities. In the process, however, the thirst for knowledge, meaning, and wisdom will lead restless and enquiring Sagittarians along all sorts of interesting byways. As the sign of "the higher mind," there is a serious side to their nature, they understand that they need their own philosophy on life and that education takes many forms.

Sagittarius and Jupiter between them have a wide range of vocational concerns. They rule higher education, and many gifted teachers, professors, or scholars are born under this sign. Editors, writers, literary agents, and publishers also belong here, as do all the legal professions, such as barristers or solicitors, and all work connected to humanitarianism, ethics, faith, and religion. Here we also find the world of professional athletics and sports, especially equestrianism as Sagittarius rules horses, being the sign of the centaur.

Jupiter and Sagittarius also rule all things foreign, including explorers, travelers, or any work linked to overseas residency or travel. Many Sagittarians find their niche in an expat community or away from their country of origin. Unsurprisingly, the entrepreneurial spirit is alive and kicking with this big-thinking sign, and they relish the freedom that money can buy. What they lack in hard experience, they will make up for with powerful intuition and visionary talents. Often there is a certain naivety and childlike trust in the world, which somehow creates luck, albeit invariably at the eleventh hour.

HEALTH

Sagittarius rules the thighs, including the femur, and the whole pelvic area, including the buttocks and sciatic nerve. They are prone to lower-back injuries that affect these parts of the body, often through sports injuries or falls. In spite of their athleticism, Sagittarians can be clumsy. They tend to look upwards rather than where they are putting their feet.

CAPRICORN (DECEMBER 23–JANUARY 20)

SYMBOL: THE MOUNTAIN GOAT
RULING PLANET: SATURN
ELEMENT AND MODE: CARDINAL EARTH
KEY PHRASE: I MASTER

SPOT THE CAPRICORN

Saturn rules all that is large, solid, slow moving, and enduring. Along with the fact that this is the sign of the hardy mountain goat, many Capricorns have strong frames, which can be either skinny and wiry or heavy set. This sign and Saturn between them rule the skeleton and most Capricorns have an excellent bone structure, particularly the cheekbones, giving them striking, unusual, and often highly photogenic faces. Think Marlene Dietrich (December 27, 1901–May 6, 1992), David Bowie (b. January 8, 1947), and Kate Moss (b. January 16, 1974). Often the face is also noticeably wide. The hair tends to be on the thin side, even when there is plenty of it, and the men often go bald relatively early in life. Young Capricorns look older than their years, but this also works the other way around. It is remarkable how many Capricorns age beautifully, becoming younger looking as they get older, compensating for looking old when they were young.

THE CAPRICORN NATURE

Saturn is the planet of age and gravitas, so this sign tends towards seriousness, often as a result of missing out on a real childhood in some way and having to grow up quickly. Learning to take responsibility for themselves, and others, is often the hallmark of Capricorns' tough start in life. Amongst my Capricorn clients we find the woman who was raised by deaf and dumb parents and who learned to be the family spokeswoman as soon as she could speak, the woman who never knew her parents and who was raised by her grandparents, subsequently feeling that she had been held back a generation, and the man whose childhood memories included taking himself to the doctor at the age of eight as a way of bypassing his mother's histrionics.

Yet, in spite of their reputation for being cautious rule-book followers and prone to pessimism, they are not always the glum and gloomy Eeyores of the zodiac. Once Capricorns break through their own reserve, they can be charming, deeply attentive, and devastatingly funny, often as a result of learning to use humor as a defense mechanism.

LOVE AND RELATIONSHIPS

A typical Capricorn prefers to build relationships carefully and gradually rather than assuming intimacy or familiarity too quickly. They observe other people's boundaries along with their own, quietly gauging reactions and responses as they get the

IN A NUTSHELL

reserved

serious

industrious

focused

pragmatic

courteous

measure of new people or new territory. They like to know where they stand, but also because they place enormous value on their personal dignity. The danger of rejection or embarrassment is especially sensitive for this sign.

Emotional risk taking is a big challenge and it can take a long time for a Capricorn to commit. The fear of intimacy can make them hold back even when they secretly long for the abandonment of wild romance. They tend to hide behind either polite conversation or, again, they will use humor to create and maintain distance by turning everything into a joke. Their ideal partner is someone who is not fooled by this or, conversely, someone who is not cowed by their sometimes-authoritative manner. The partner who knows how to find the child within the Capricorn man or woman—and bring it out to play—has a playmate and lover for life.

VOCATION

The mountain goat is purposeful and surefooted, able to pick its way up even the craggiest of rock faces. This reflects the legendary Capricorn ambition, which is arguably top of the textbook keywords for this sign, but in reality their deeply ingrained work ethic takes many different forms. Not all Capricorns want to run their own company or take up positions of power. More accurately, Capricorns are goal orientated and generally love to have a project on the go, to have their plans mapped out clearly and realistically, to know what they are doing, when they are doing it, and why. They do not do pointlessness. Whether it is doing the supermarket shopping or empire building, there is always a clear objective.

As Saturn rules all structures, including hierarchy, and is the planet of work, effort, and respectability, it is hardly surprising that many Capricorns are nevertheless to be found in top managerial posts, government offices, or at the helm of their own businesses. They are talented at taking the sentiment out of the picture, driving a hard bargain, and are motivated by results. This sign also rules mining, building, and architecture, but whatever the profession, the aim is always to build, achieve, and secure. Many Capricorns also find success in later life as they start reclaiming the missed opportunities of their youth.

HEALTH

The built-for-endurance Capricorn has stamina and a great deal of resilience. They tend not to suffer unduly from all bugs and are generally blessed with a brilliant immune system. Even when they are ill, they tend to bear their aches and pains with stoicism. However, everyone has their vulnerable spots, and for Capricorn it is the bones, especially the knees. Generally, Capricorn is linked to the process of hardening so also rules the teeth, hair, nails, and cell walls. The correct calcium intake is crucial for this sign. As Saturn symbolizes boundaries, this planet and Capricorn also both rule the skin, the boundary of the physical body. Painful and difficult-to-treat afflictions such as osteoporosis, arthritis, eczema, and psoriasis all belong to the Saturn-Capricorn domain.

Textbook
CAPRICORNS

Greek shipping magnate **Aristotle Onassis** (January 20, 1906–March 15, 1975) was the ultimate empire builder. A childhood of riches to rags, due to his prestigious family becoming refugees, did not stop him from making his first million by the age of 25.

In addition to their own "make good" streak, Capricorn women are often attracted to partners in prestigious roles. **Catherine Middleton**, the Duchess of Cambridge (b. January 9, 1982), clearly made a love match but also married into a lifetime of rules, duty, and service.

Actor, comedian, and producer **Jim Carrey** (b. January 17, 1962) worked full time rather than finishing high school to help his family through financial hardship and to care for his chronically ill mother. The child in him is the hallmark of his work and on set his professional approach is said to be, "Let's have fun. Let's play in the sandbox."

AQUARIUS

SYMBOL: THE WATER BEARER

RULING PLANET: SATURN   CO-RULER: URANUS

ELEMENT AND MODE: FIXED AIR

KEY PHRASE: I UNDERSTAND

SPOT THE AQUARIUS

As two very different planets rule this sign between them, so are there two distinct types of Aquarians. The Saturn type is conservative and tends to dress down, even for a special occasion. Favorite items get worn until they drop into holes and indulgence is frowned upon, so the women tend to eschew makeup or jewelry. The Uranus type is the opposite, experimenting with styles and colors, regardless of what may be in fashion. They take pride in their own unique look, which sometimes comes off as flamboyant or eccentric, and often stand out in a crowd. In the physical body, Aquarius rules the lower leg and ankles, and the women, in particular, tend to have long legs and lovely slender ankles. Aquarius also rules the circulation and this sign usually suffers from the cold. Look for the person huddled in a sweater on a warm day. Also look for stunning eyes, often a piercing metallic blue in Uranian types.

THE AQUARIUS NATURE

Much can be learned about the Sun signs by considering the nature of opposites. The blazing fire sign of Leo prizes individuality, but Aquarius is the voice of the collective. The immediate paradox with this sign is that, although they are the sign of the group, they often struggle to "fit in." It is unusual to find an Aquarian who has not had the experience of feeling deeply "different" from their peers, even from a very early age. Often, there is a childhood story of feeling misunderstood or sidelined, or of being raised in a family culture of strict rules or emotional neglect.

Quirky, unusual, curious, and usually of above average intelligence, an Aquarian tends to make sense of the world through logic rather than feelings. Organized, systematic, compulsive list makers, placing great value on their own particular way of doing things, these individuals have strong and often unshakeable convictions. Never enter into an argument or a heated debate thinking for one moment that you will win. As Aquarian astrologer and one of my first teachers. the late Derek Appleby, once said to me, "Virgos think they are right, Aquarians know they are right!" Or in the words of another Aquarian friend, "it's not me who is strange, it's everyone else."

LOVE AND RELATIONSHIPS

The textbooks tell us that Aquarians are cold, detached, and lacking in empathy. While it is true that they can definitely give this impression, and some Aquarians do end up closing down a lot of their feelings or never fully recover from early repression, you can rest assured that more usually there is a turmoil bubbling behind

IN A NUTSHELL

systematic

impartial

inquisitive

friendly

humane

original

the cool mask of indifference. Some of the most emotional people I have ever known are Aquarians, but they definitely take a lot of getting to know.

The journey from friendliness to true intimacy is a long one for this complex sign. Saturnian types, in particular, are easily embarrassed or uncomfortable with displays of emotion and can be disconnected from their own authentic feelings. They crave union yet they create distance, often by giving out the wrong signals of superiority, inflexibility, or militant independence. Uranian types can also be intransigent but are more gregarious, easily embracing the unconventional and attaching huge importance to their many and varied friendships.

Unsurprisingly, then, Aquarians, especially, need time to build trust and understanding, and successful partnership tends to spring from friendship first, lust second. A true meeting of minds is crucial for this sign and, even when a relationship breaks up, Aquarians tend to keep ex-lovers and partners as friends whenever possible. Emotional bonds, once forged, foster a touching and steadfast loyalty.

VOCATION

Aquarius is objective and stands for the bigger picture of society, the planet, and the world at large. Communism and organizations such as Greenpeace, Amnesty International, and Médecins Sans Frontières can all be said to be Aquarian. Inside every Aquarian is a conscience, a sense of definite right and wrong, a moralist, a rebel, or a philanthropist, so any work that is aimed at the greater good has their name all over it. This is where the Aquarian low-on-drama streak works most effectively, on causes that need brain power rather than purely an emotional reaction.

Along with humanitarian, ecological, and revolutionary concerns, many Aquarians are also to be found in political offices, social work, or teaching roles, especially those linked to minorities or special needs. With their disciplined nature and appreciation of structure and systems, they are also able administrators, making good team players or leaders within large companies or departments. With Uranus' link to technology, many Aquarians are also drawn to the world of IT and inventions. Thanks to their curiosity, brilliance, and being ahead of their time, this is where we find the mad professor archetype, producing geniuses, scientists, and original thinkers.

HEALTH

Aquarius rules the legs, especially the lower legs and the ankles, and all accidents or afflictions affecting these parts of the body. It also rules circulation of the blood, and this sign often suffers from the cold or circulatory problems. Metaphorically, this links to Aquarians' reputation for coolness and can signal the need to create warmth, cosiness, and passion in their lives.

Regular exercise too benefits this sign. With their intellect, there is a risk of living too much in their heads and neglecting the body. Psychotherapy and counseling in any form are also powerful tools for channeling their busy brains along the neural pathways to good mental health and the avoidance of nervous ailments.

PISCES

(FEBRUARY 20–MARCH 20)

SYMBOL: THE FISH
RULING PLANET: JUPITER   CO-RULER: NEPTUNE
ELEMENT AND MODE: MUTABLE WATER
KEY PHRASE: I REDEEM

SPOT THE PISCES

The typical Piscean bears a striking facial resemblance to their symbol the fish. Note the wide, full-cheeked faces that usually run to fleshiness, especially in later years. Look for the generous, full-lipped mouth, dreamy, glinting eyes set wide apart that are often soft to the extent of being doe-eyed and sometimes protruding. Those same sensitive eyes easily brim with tears at sad stories or hurtful comments. Often, there is something ethereal about Pisces, either in their beauty or in the way that they move, sometimes giving the impression of being disconnected from their physical body. This sign rules the feet, and they often have a distinctive walk.

Sea colors are favorites—greens, blues, and aquamarines—and the style is often bohemian, romantic, or artistic rather than conventional. Even in a suit a Piscean would find a way of softening the edges and adding a dash of glamour.

THE PISCES NATURE

As the sign of mutable water and co-ruled by Neptune, god of the sea, so is the Piscean nature free flowing. Their own personalities are somehow boundless and it is rare to find a Pisces of the seriously shy and retiring kind beyond childhood. They are often larger than life and hugely entertaining and charismatic, both in social and work scenarios. Both sexes tend to follow their instincts, to "go with the flow," and usually have a horror of being confined, contained, or controlled.

There is a raw vulnerability to this sign, especially in their early, defenseless years. Their fellow water signs—the Scorpion with its sting and the Crab with its shell and pincers—have their attack and defense mechanisms, but the Fish has no protection other than to wriggle away and swim faster than anyone else. In this respect, Pisceans can be elusive, evasive, indirect, insincere, or paranoid.

Like water, Pisces will take the shape of the vessel, easily or unconsciously fitting into other people's moulds and expectations. If they confuse you, that is nothing compared to what they do to themselves. Finding their own firm sense of self is possibly their biggest challenge.

LOVE AND RELATIONSHIPS

Sensitive, imaginative, sympathetic on one hand, wounded, distrustful, and suspicious on the other, the arena of personal intimacy can be an emotional minefield for this multifaceted sign. Relationships are usually built with a great deal of testing the water before taking the plunge and before revealing their true and innermost persona.

IN A NUTSHELL

sensitive

empathic

artistic

addictive

instinctive

visionary

Pisceans are also natural rescuers. They will do anything for you, especially if you are in genuine need. They are also great at getting you to do things for them, in a subtle way that is not immediately obvious. To one extent or another, there is a manipulative streak in every Pisces that they have to learn not to exploit, if only to avoid sabotaging the goal of building the authentic relationships that they need.

The attraction to those who suffer and the collapse of personal boundaries can unfortunately lead to all kinds of relationship disasters. Often their own need to be rescued is projected on to others, and the lesson to be learned is that they cannot heal a lover's early trauma or support the struggling artist forever. In romance they are far more likely to find happiness with someone with bags of common sense, who can provide emotional security and be their rock in life.

VOCATION

Dreamy Pisceans often struggle with the realities of day-to-day life on dry land. They have to figure out how to satisfy their creative appetites as well as pay the bills. Once they find their way upstream, they can achieve great things, but until this turn is made, they can only splash around in the shallows, small fish in big ponds. It is vital for Pisceans, however, to find their true vocation. Although they are highly adaptable, the grind of the average, soulless nine-to-five can make them depressed or ill. Usually they are born with a natural gift, something innate that could never be taught.

Inside every Pisces is a thespian struggling to get out. Many wonderful actors are born under this sign, they can be whoever you want them to be, and you can also add an astounding number of theatre workers, musicians, writers, artists, and poets to the list.

Pisces' connection to compassion, suffering, and sacrifice shows in the domain of work connected to charities and places of confinement, such as refuges, hospitals, or prisons. Pubs, bars, the liquor trade, and all marine work also belong to this sign.

HEALTH

Pisces is the sign of escapism, the retreat from the painful demands of a harsh world. This can take the form of meditation or mysticism but, as this sign also rules alcohol, drugs, and all altered states of consciousness, Pisceans are especially at risk of alcoholism or substance abuse. Like the other exuberant Jupiter sign of Sagittarius, they find it hard to hit the brake pedal, but Sagittarians tend to do this in the spirit of joie de vivre, whereas Pisceans are more likely to drown their sorrows. Conversely, alcohol abuse in the family history can be the root of deep damage. The single most effective health remedy for this sign is to learn how to step out of the victim role.

In the physical body, Pisces rules the lymphatic system and the feet. Apart from injury, problems include in-growing toenails, bunions, or deformities from wearing ill-fitting shoes in childhood. Many Piscean women, in particular, have a love affair with shoes, or hate them, the latter often arising from difficulty in finding anything to fit them properly.

THE ELEMENTS AND MODES

♈ ♉ ♊ ♋ ♌ ♍

Think of the horoscope as an onion. Sun signs are the outer wrapper, covering many other layers that lead us into the heart of any individual chart. The natural symmetry of the horoscope, and the realization that everything in astrology is connected, starts to unfold as soon as we look at the Sun signs in terms of the distribution of elements and modes.

The assignment of an element and mode further singularizes the signs, illustrating and refining their essential temperament and the ways in which this is expressed.

ELEMENTS

The four astrological elements are fire, earth, air, and water. Every fourth sign shares the same element, so there are three signs for each. These are known as the triplicities.

THE FIRE TRIPLICITY
Aries, Leo, Sagittarius

THE EARTH TRIPLICITY
Taurus, Virgo, Capricorn

THE AIR TRIPLICITY
Gemini, Libra, Aquarius

THE WATER TRIPLICITY
Cancer, Scorpio, Pisces

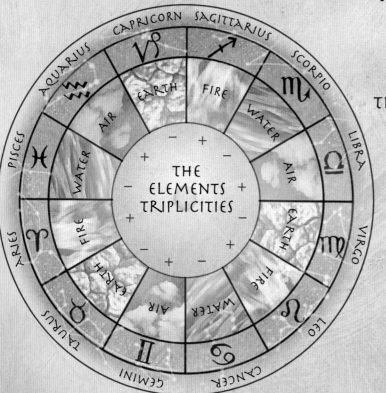

CHARACTERISTICS

If you join up any three signs of the same triplicity, you will create an equilateral triangle. This is the first stepping stone towards understanding aspects—the relationship between signs—as detailed in Chapter Four. For now, note that signs sharing the same element are in trine with one another, that is, they are compatible or harmonious—think "being in your element."

FIRE
warmth, passion, vision, intuition

EARTH
sensuality, practicality, fertility, materialism

AIR
thought, intellect, ideas, interaction

WATER
feelings, sensitivity, empathy, instinct

Swiss psychiatrist and psychotherapist Carl Jung had a lifelong interest in astrology. The four cognitive functions of the psyche, which he conceived originally, correlate directly with the four elements. The links between the psyche and the elements can be delineated as follows:

FIRE INTUITION Intuitives find meaning through what may be termed non-rational information, such as hunches or visions. They can make leaps of imagination or connect their insights in a way that leads to "I just know" answers.

EARTH SENSATION Sensates find meaning through rational information as gathered through the five senses of sight, taste, touch, sound, and smell. Their world is one of concrete reality in which a sixth sense is either absent or disregarded.

AIR THINKING Thinkers find meaning through rational information, such as facts and figures. They operate by what makes sense; they look for logical connections and are disorientated by people or matters that they cannot understand.

WATER FEELING Feelers find meaning through non-rational information and operate purely on the basis of how someone or something makes them feel. They react emotionally and base their judgments on pleasant or unpleasant impressions.

MODES

The three astrological modes are cardinal, fixed, and mutable. Every third sign shares the same mode, so there are four signs for each. These are known as the quadruplicities.

If you join up any four signs of the same quadruplicity, you will create a square. For now note that signs sharing the same mode are in "square" to one another and are incompatible or inharmonious.

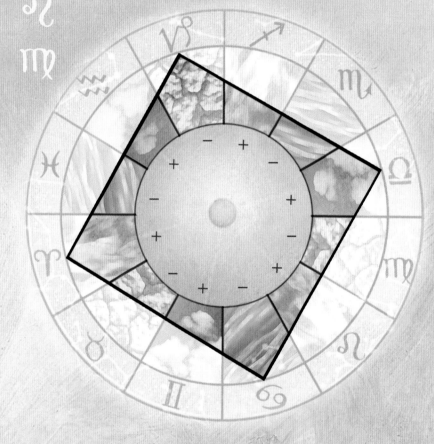

CARDINAL

This mode represents the element in its most concentrated or active form. It is associated with push, energy, and initiation.

FIXED

As the name suggests, this mode represents the element in its least changeable form. It is associated with stability or stubbornness.

MUTABLE

Sometimes called "common," this mode represents the element at its most fluid. It is associated with flexibility, movement, and the dissemination of energy.

Note

Every fire and air sign is masculine and every earth and water sign is feminine. These are also referred to as positive or negative but not in any "good or bad" sense—think yin-yang energy, which describes how opposite forces are not only complementary but also interdependent. In the same way, the Sun and Moon are another example, as it would be impossible to have night without day.

IN A NUTSHELL

Aries: Cardinal Fire, masculine

Taurus: Fixed Earth, feminine

Gemini: Mutable Air, masculine

Cancer: Cardinal Water, feminine

Leo: Fixed Fire, masculine

Virgo: Mutable Earth, feminine

Libra: Cardinal Air, masculine

Scorpio: Fixed Water, feminine

Sagittarius: Mutable Fire, masculine

Capricorn: Cardinal Earth, feminine

Aquarius: Fixed Air, masculine

Pisces: Mutable Water, feminine

CHAPTER 2
THE PLANETS

Sun signs can be thought-provokingly accurate, but in many ways
they are but the tip of the iceberg, the outer layer of the onion.
The real depth and complexity of horoscopy start to emerge
when we introduce the other planets. The first seven heavenly
bodies—the Sun, Moon, Mercury, Venus, Mars, Jupiter, and
Saturn—are known as the Personal Planets (see p. 54). They are
followed by the outer, much slower-moving planets of Uranus,
Neptune, and Pluto. Modern-day astrology now also includes the
minor planet Chiron, which was discovered in 1977.

THE SYMBOLISM OF THE PLANETS

R is the glyph to denote retrograde motion. If you see the initials "SR" after a planet, this stands for Stationary Retrograde, meaning that the planet is switching on that very day from direct to retrograde motion. If you see the initials "SD" after a planet, this stands for Stationary Direct, meaning that the reverse is happening and that the planet is switching from retrograde to direct motion.

Astronomically, of course, planets do not literally stop and turn around but, in terms of our line of vision from the earth, there are periods when they appear to do so. Apart from the Sun and the Moon, all the planets spend periods of time in retrograde motion. The further away from the Sun, the longer the period of retrograde motion.

Astrologically, retrograde motion indicates that the symbolic message and purpose of the planet in question is in some way concealed, obscured, or delayed.

Every planet has a sign or signs that it rules. These are also known as the planet's sign(s) of dignity. The natures of the planet/sign are complementary and work together harmoniously. The opposite sign(s) are the planet's sign of detriment, in which the natures of the planet/sign are in conflict and struggle to understand each other. Note that this does not necessarily mean a simple split between "good" and "bad," as you will find when you read through the following interpretations, but rather that there exists some friction or potential for conflict. Every (personal) planet also has a sign in which it is said to be exalted, where it is arguably at its strongest placing. The sign opposite the sign of exaltation is the (personal) planet's sign of fall, its weakest placing, in which the natures of the planet/sign are mostly a mystery to each other.

Much astrological interpretation in terms of the natal chart (the horoscope) lies in assessing the combination of planets in signs. This works at many levels, but there are two major strands to planetary symbolism:

UNIVERSAL

What the planet stands for at a general level. For example, Mercury rules everything that comes under the umbrella of communication.

PARTICULAR

What the planet symbolizes in any given chart. For example, if you have Mercury in Aries, the nature of communication is fast, direct, and to the point. If you have Mercury in the opposite sign of Libra, the nature of communication is more discursive and seeks opinions.

Crucially, the "particular" also includes other people. The art of horoscopy really starts to open up when we ask not just "what is this planet" but "who is this planet?" So the horoscope does not just delineate personality characteristics but also the nature of our relationships and those who people our world.

The following cameos of the planets through the twelve signs are offered as "takes," that is, illustrations as opposed to absolute givens, snapshots of symbolism as seen through my own client work or in the lives of prominent people. As with the Sun signs in the opening chapter, we are primarily considering the nature of the planet in a sign in isolation rather than within the context of any particular horoscope. Therefore, the characteristics may run very true to type, or they may be modified, for good or ill, depending on the planet's position within the chart and its relationship to the other planets. In these cameos you will come across mentions of the houses of the zodiac, degree-positions, and Ascendants; these finer details make up the next two, deeper, layers of the onion, and are unpeeled and explored at length in Chapters Three and Four.

PLANET		DIGNITY	DETRIMENT	EXALTATION	FALL
☉	Sun	Leo	Aquarius	Aries	Libra
☽	Moon	Cancer	Capricorn	Taurus	Scorpio
☿	Mercury	Gemini Virgo	Sagittarius Pisces	Virgo	Pisces
♀	Venus	Taurus Libra	Scorpio Aries	Pisces	Virgo
♂	Mars	Aries Scorpio	Libra Taurus	Capricorn	Cancer
♃	Jupiter	Sagittarius Pisces	Gemini Virgo	Cancer	Capricorn
♄	Saturn	Capricorn Aquarius	Cancer Leo	Libra	Aries
♅	Uranus	Co-ruler of Aquarius	Leo	None	None
♆	Neptune	Co-ruler of Pisces	Virgo	None	None
♇	Pluto	Co-ruler of Scorpio	Taurus	None	None
⚷	Chiron	Possible co-ruler of Sagittarius	Gemini	None	None

THE MOON

SIGN OF DIGNITY: CANCER
COLORS: SILVER AND WHITE
DAY OF THE WEEK: MONDAY
METAL: SILVER

MOON
Herbs and Foods

Lunar herbs and foods are cooling, drying, or sleep inducing. These include cucumber, coriander, moonwort, pumpkin, cabbage, lettuce, and watercress.

In traditional astrology, the Sun is Lord of the Day and the Moon is Lady of the Night, known together as the Luminaries or the Lights. The masculine Sun symbolizes our day world, the essential self, consciousness, and the life force, whereas the feminine Moon symbolizes our night world and the power of the unconscious. She also rules women, mothers and babies, our childhood, and fertility.

The Moon symbolizes our emotions, instincts, needs, and habitual responses, along with our home, as well as early family life. Often she will describe the mother's nature and character, and therefore the kind of mothering and emotional imprinting we received. If you want to understand the feeling nature, to find the little boy or girl within the man or woman, then the Moon is where to start.

MOON IN ARIES

As the first sign of the zodiac and ruled by the action planet Mars, being "top" is what Aries does best. This Moon symbolizes the pioneering nature, the need to lead—and excel. Both Bill Gates (b. October 28, 1955) of Microsoft and the late Steve Jobs (February 24, 1955–October 5, 2011) of Apple have this Moon in their sign, and their work has changed the face of technology forever. Supermodel Tyra Banks (b. December 4, 1973) moved beyond the catwalk and started her own production company, which went on to produce *America's Next Top Model*, *The X Factor* of the modeling world. Tyra acted as host, judge, and executive producer.

Aries rules the self, and psychologically this is a young and "self"-ish, "me first" Moon. Its problem-side is the child or teenage-ego state, which is preoccupied with its own needs. The self-esteem pendulum swings from an egotistical sense of personal entitlement to a deeply ingrained and powerful self-belief. When the balance is found and the Aries fire is channeled into true autonomy, the full power of this Moon's awesome single-mindedness comes into its own.

As with the Sun in Aries, many Aries Moon women go through their "red phase," such as Piscean Rihanna (b. February 20, 1988). She constantly reinvents her image but arguably one of her most memorable looks remains that of her cascade of red curls.

IN A NUTSHELL **efficient, impatient, assured.**

MOON IN TAURUS EXALTATION

With the Moon's 28-day cycle and connection to women, conception, and nurturing, it makes symbolic sense to find that she is exalted in the fixed and fertile earth sign of Taurus. Here, all the lunar sensitivity and changeability is held, contained, and nourished. Individuals with this Moon often have strong family roots and a deep connection with one or both parents. As a result, they, in turn, tend to take to parenting in a natural and hands-on way. The emotional nature is generally contented and not given to drama. They have a great deal of perseverance and do not mind getting their hands dirty.

This is also Prince Charles' Moon (b. November 14, 1948). He is known for his love of agriculture and for being a pioneer of organic farming. Furthermore, this is the perfect symbolic showing of the Moon's sign of exaltation in regards to women and family. His mother, the Queen (b. April 21, 1926), is a Taurus, and he will forever be linked to the exalted Diana, herself carrying the name of the Roman goddess of the Moon and birth. Charles and Diana's children, in turn, have powerful Moons—William (b. June 21, 1982) has the Moon dignified in Cancer (Cancer also being Diana's Sun sign) and Harry (b. September 15, 1984) has the Moon exalted in Taurus.

TAURUS

IN A NUTSHELL **sensual, secure, down to earth.**

MOON IN GEMINI

The Moon in Mercury's masculine sign bestows liveliness and quickness, often expressed by a childlike or impish quality, a sense of fun, and slapstick humor. Being big kids themselves, they have a natural understanding of children and how to enter into a child's world. Note the mobility to the features and a lack of self-consciousness that is part of playing the fool, mimicry, and an "up for anything" attitude. Goldie Hawn (b. November 21, 1945), Jim Carrey (b. January 17, 1962), and Rowan Atkinson (b. January 6, 1955) all have this Moon.

The link to language often shows through rapid speech, a penchant for writing or media work, or cleverness with words, such as master of wit Groucho Marx (October 2, 1890–August 19, 1977). Look, too, for the Gemini duality. Actress Gwyneth Paltrow (b. September 27, 1972) is bilingual, speaking fluent Spanish, and is raising her children to be bilingual. Dexterity is also a characteristic. Amongst my own Moon Gemini clients is a primary school teacher turned theatrical seamstress, a job at which she excels.

The duality may show in early upbringing, such as two homes or two sets of parents. This is also one of the archetypes of the womanizer or the person who leads a double life. Hollywood legend Spencer Tracy (April 5, 1900–June 10, 1967) remained officially married to Louise Treadwell, but his affair with Katharine Hepburn lasted 26 years. This Moon definitely needs stimulus and variety. Often, there is a wide and eclectic circle of friends and a larger than usual repertoire of outside interests.

IN A NUTSHELL **curious, adaptable, mischievous.**

CANCER

MOON IN CANCER DIGNITY

The Moon is at home in Cancer, sign of family, parenting, and homemaking. Cancer's concerns of procreation and protection dovetail with the lunar qualities of nurturing, caring, and containing. However, this does not mean that all Cancer-Moon people automatically have an easy or secure start in life. Early home life can either be an emotional idyll, or there is some story of an overly sheltered upbringing or a wounding relationship with one or both parents. One of my clients comes from a large family of six children, with a caring but reserved father and a mother who seemed incapable of attending to anyone's needs other than her own. All of the children learned from an early age to look after one another and none of them developed an adult relationship with their mother that went beyond pure duty.

However, whether life started with neglect or with strong family roots and support, these Moon people tend to place enormous value on their own home and have a nurturing streak that will express itself in some obvious way. Either they prove to be natural family makers or they channel their care into fostering, nursing, animals, or a charity. Psychiatrist Elisabeth Kübler-Ross (July 8, 1926–August 24, 2004) was a "double" Cancer, having both the Sun and the Moon in this sign, and is famous for revolutionizing the way that the medical profession treated the terminally ill. Her dream of building a hospice for infants and children with HIV sadly was thwarted by the ignorance of local residents.

IN A NUTSHELL clannish, encouraging, sympathetic.

MOON IN LEO

The Moon in the Sun's sign is perfect symbolism for a female monarch—this is Queen Elizabeth II's Moon—and there is something "royal" in the manner of all these individuals. Every Leo Moon needs its adoring public and special attention. If you are in a relationship with a Leo-Moon person, you can get away with anything, as long as you spoil them, appreciate them, and worship the ground on which they walk. The moment they feel as if they are no longer Top Cat, the relationship usually withers and dies.

At work and at home these Moon people are central, competent, and efficient. You can throw pretty much anything at them and, after the initial drama, they will step into their creative mode and find a way to cope. They believe wholeheartedly in their own abilities and, as a result, tend towards bossiness. When it comes to giving orders, they like to be in charge, rather than on the receiving end, and do not take kindly to being told what to do. They loathe being ridiculed and the knee-jerk response to any embarrassment is to stand on their dignity.

Philippa "Pippa" Middleton (b. September 6, 1983), sister to Catherine, Duchess of Cambridge, has the Moon at 29 degrees of Leo, the position of a fixed star called Regulus—known as the royal star and associated with supreme success and recognition. This symbolizes her own elevated status as sister to the future queen and that of her creative (Leo) mother (Moon) who made a fortune through her own party (Leo/fifth house) business.

IN A NUTSHELL **commanding, affectionate, organized.**

MOON IN VIRGO

The Moon in Mercury's feminine sign is more complicated than it seems. Early stories include parents who set impossibly high standards, working parents who never had enough time for their children, and children never feeling good enough or having to win love through achievements. Often they battle with the ingrained belief that they are unlovable when in fact it was their parents who were unloving. One of my Moon-Virgo clients traced many of her problems back to her mother, who was the ultimate housewife, investing all of her energy into keeping a perfect home and holding lavish dinner parties for her top-businessman husband. This fits perfectly with the Moon (mother) in Virgo (perfection and service) in a routine that was sacrosanct. Even my client's suicide attempt in her troubled teens was, in her belief, interpreted and treated as a massive inconvenience, causing her mother intense embarrassment. The Moon rules mirrors and illusion, so the real issue was that she had shattered the image of the perfect family.

VIRGO

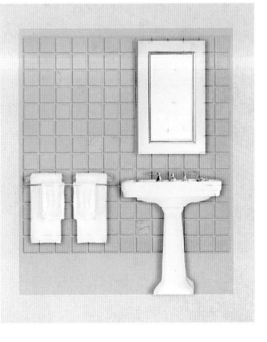

This, of course, is one of the worst-case scenarios, but it illustrates the very sensitive and complex needs of this Moon. The Virgo tendency to pick things apart can make the emotional life a hard one and eating disorders are a common problem. These individuals need gentleness, unwavering approval, and acceptance. They also thrive on routine when it is not too obsessive. Just do not move their things around—they will notice the slightest item out of place—or leave the bathroom in a mess. They may be overly fastidious and fretful but, when happy, they are delightful, witty, deeply insightful, and, when you are in need, they are the first to come to the rescue.

IN A NUTSHELL **vulnerable, meticulous, observant.**

MOON IN LIBRA

The Moon in the Venus-ruled sign of the Scales learns about relating from a very early age. Good parenting teaches equality and sharing skills in a home environment that is safe and harmonious, enabling the child to enter adult life with emotional maturity and healthy self-esteem. These qualities are exceptionally important for this Moon as "the other"—the other side of the Scales—is a primary need. The opposite experience, when a child learns that others always come first, can have disastrous consequences, fostering enfeebling dependency and a "someone is better than no one" approach to their love life.

One of my Moon-Libra clients, now in her fifties, has never spent more than a few weeks out of a relationship. In spite of my frequent assurances that she would naturally meet and attract new partners, she has never been able to put this to the test. After every break up, it is straight back to online dating sites and ads. When these Moon people turn into serial daters, it flags up the real issue of needing some single time in order to discover their own true sense of self.

Libra's link to beauty and fashion is also important, and these individuals need to feel relaxed in their home or office and happy with their looks, clothes, and accessories. Usually there is an eye for style, and some of the world's most famous designers have this Moon, including Louis Vuitton (August 4, 1821–February 27, 1892), Pierre Cardin (b. July 2, 1927), Hubert de Givenchy (b. February 21, 1927), and Miuccia Prada (b. May 10, 1949).

LIBRA

IN A NUTSHELL **unassertive, peaceable, adaptable.**

MOON IN SCORPIO FALL

Note that Mars thrives in Scorpio where the Moon is at her most vulnerable. Then throw in the fact that Scorpio is also co-ruled by all-or-nothing Pluto, planet of power, sex, death, and rebirth, and you begin to have a taste of what Moon-in-Scorpio people are up against. Formative experiences amongst my own clients include early bereavement, the wicked stepmother, being rigidly controlled, or suffering abuse.

These Moon people absolutely have to find their own power or, in return, they can abuse or self-destruct. Often this means rebellion or flying in the face of convention in order to embark upon the healing journey. Author and publisher Louise Hay (b. October 8, 1926) was raped at age five, dropped out of school, had a teenage pregnancy, and, when she turned 16, gave up her baby daughter for adoption. Gynecological problems are common for women with this Moon sign—in her early fifties, Louise was diagnosed with "incurable" cervical cancer. She refused conventional treatment and cured herself. She is now world famous for her book *You Can Heal Your Life*, which investigates the physical and metaphysical nature of disease.

Nancy Friday (b. August 27, 1933) also embodies the awesome "powerful woman" archetype of this Moon. She exploded the taboo around women's sexual fantasies with her first book *My Secret Garden*, and explored the psychology of guilt about sex that women hand down to one another in *My Mother/My Self*.

A psychologically and spiritually enriched life is possibly this Moon's paramount need. The gift of deep insight often extends into psychic abilities, too. This is also Nostradamus' Moon (December 14, 1503–July 2, 1566).

IN A NUTSHELL **wounded, resilient, transformational.**

MOON IN SAGITTARIUS

The Moon in Jupiter's masculine sign is cheerful, immediately friendly, and often a rolling stone. With a natural clownish streak, they make for hugely entertaining company and can break the ice at the most stilted of occasions. You would pay them to come to your party.

Truth is a big issue for this Moon but, unlike the Sun Sagittarian, they do not always pursue it at the cost of all else. The knee-jerk reaction of steering clear of anything "heavy" can make them shy away from deep truths, about themselves, their partners, or their upbringing. They would rather not admit that their mother fell hopelessly short of noticing their real needs and the "ignorance is bliss" option enables their denial.

SAGITTARIUS

When the inevitable crisis arrives, usually in later life, they wake up to the fact that happiness is inextricably linked with self-awareness. After a love affair went devastatingly wrong, one woman in her late forties went on a learning mission, signing up for residential therapy courses and reading everything she could get her hands on. There is no doubt in my mind that she saved her own mental health. At the other extreme, I once lent a Moon-Sagittarius guy the insightful Dorothy Rowe book *Beyond Fear*. He read the first page in my presence and announced, open mouthed, "Oh my god, this could have been written for me!" He returned it three months later, unread.

Emigrating, periods of living abroad, or, especially for the men, living with a foreign partner are also common stories for this Moon.

IN A NUTSHELL **engaging, spirited, unbiased.**

MOON IN CAPRICORN DETRIMENT

Note that any Moon–Saturn combination is tricky, as signaled by their conflicting signs of dignity and detriment:

- The Moon is dignified in Cancer, Saturn's sign of detriment.
- The Moon is in detriment in Capricorn, Saturn's sign of dignity.

It is not always easy to connect with the real person behind this Moon. On the surface, they are charm personified, often with an old-world-type courtesy or chivalry. They listen intently and take a serious interest in everything you say. It is only when the conversation is over that you realize that they have volunteered virtually nothing personal. Feelings are markedly compartmentalized and some doors remain firmly closed and locked, even to themselves.

The textbooks would have you believe that these Moon people are cold, unfeeling, and incapable of affection. This is a misrepresentation. More typically, there is nearly always some early situation, which, in some way, forced them to grow up too quickly. Tennis star Maria Sharapova's (b. April 19, 1987) story is a textbook example. Her father embodied the parent as main carer (Moon), with ambition and responsibility (Capricorn) for his child prodigy, borrowing money to get them both to the US, and then slaving away at any job he could get. The absent mothering was a consequence of this, as visa restrictions prevented Maria's mother from joining them for two years.

My own clients include the man whose mother died when he was only 13, just as he was entering adolescence, and the woman whose "childhood" revolved around her mother's alcoholism. As a result of such upbringings, this Moon often signals a truncated childhood , placing the individual at a distinct disadvantage with regard to acquiring intimacy skills. Choosing an older person as a life partner, especially the men, is a common occurrence for this Moon.

IN A NUTSHELL **private, honorable, self-reliant.**

MOON IN AQUARIUS

The Moon in Saturn's masculine sign, with innovative and new-age Uranus as co-ruler, is a mixed bag. The Saturn type is deadly logical, objective, and sometimes distant. The Uranus type is more avant-garde with progressive or unconventional ideas about relationships. Both types, especially when struggling through adolescence, are not sure whether they should have feelings at all. They tend to over-rationalize or minimize their emotional needs and reactions and, consequently, those of others. Early upbringing experiences are often about a family culture that places huge value on academic achievement or the "stiff upper lip," parenting that provides the basic needs of survival but goes no further, or parents who operate by a strict rulebook. The best-case early scenario for this Moon is of parents who walk the talk, who practice equality and fairness, and who are their child's best friends.

In spite of Aquarius being the sign of groups, these individuals often struggle with shyness and feeling different. They need to fit in, yet they often go through periods of being head-in-the-clouds loners. In love, possibly their biggest challenge is to heal the split between the theory and practice of personal relationships. However, this Moon is low on drama, and, as confidence grows, they usually find happiness when the focus is on friendship and a true meeting of minds. At a wider level, they need the company of those who share their intellectual interests.

Moon in Aquarius is also about the collective and the needs of a country. Many successful politicians have this Moon, including former Prime Minister Tony Blair (b. May 6, 1951) and Chancellor of Germany, Angela Merkel (b. July 17, 1954).

IN A NUTSHELL **brisk, brilliant, humane.**

MOON IN PISCES

All of the water signs operate on their feelings, but the Moon in Jupiter's feminine sign is possibly the most sensitive combination of all. Even more than the Sun in this sign, these individuals have very thin skins and are easily wounded. Traditional astrology teaches that Pisces is the sign of suffering, sacrifice, or loss, and often there is a difficult start in life connected to these themes.

Co-ruled by Neptune, god of the boundless seas, these Moon people seek fusion but, in fact, need firm and clear boundaries. Without them, life is disillusioning, painful, and characterized by escapism, sometimes through being loners or through alcohol or drugs. Their demons are despondency, self-pity, or paranoia. In love they idealize and can feel overwhelmingly crushed when the loved one inevitably topples off their pedestal. Psychologically, they may have missed out on a healthy "separation" phase in childhood, which results in issues around where they stop and other people begin.

At best, there is pronounced artistic talent, generosity, and the ability to empathize on a phenomenal scale. One of my Moon-Pisces clients, without knowing anything about astrology, is a spot on example of how people "speak their chart." Her own words capture the imagery of mutable water and the empathic and sacrificial nature:

"I like to look into a person's eyes and know I've made them happy. More, I want that person to be overflowing with happiness. I have made a person feel good by giving them something of mine I value, it's hurt me to give it away but, when I see the happiness, it's worth the loss."

IN A NUTSHELL **receptive, impressionable, kind.**

MERCURY

SIGNS OF DIGNITY: GEMINI AND VIRGO
COLOR: ALL THAT IS MIXED OR MULTICOLORED
DAY OF THE WEEK: WEDNESDAY
METAL: QUICKSILVER

MERCURY
Herbs and Foods

Carrots, celery, mushrooms, myrtle, parsley, dill, fennel, and lavender. Peppermint, rich in menthol with soothing and antibacterial properties, also belongs to Mercury, as does the mildly sedative valerian.

Mercury is Hermes, winged messenger of the gods, and thus he rules communication and everything related to the spoken or written word. Phones, computers, e-mails and all other correspondence, the media, books, diaries, and information in all its guises are Mercury's realm. He is our voice and our words, not just what we say, but how we say it and what we sound like.

As planet of the mind, he governs our thought processes, too, including ideas, opinions, attitudes, and beliefs. He rules youth and early learning, so he has a say in how our outlook and world view are shaped and influenced in our formative years.

Mercury rules the hands and dexterity and is therefore the archetype of the magician or trickster and thief.

MERCURY IN ARIES

If you want to get the vibe of Mercury in speed-freak Mars' sign, then look no further than Anita Renfroe (b. April 4, 1962). She was born on a New Moon in Aries as well as having Mercury in this sign. Her song "Momisms" condenses everything a mother would say into less than three minutes, and she belts it out to the breakneck tune of the William Tell overture. It made her a YouTube sensation.

This Mercury thinks in straight lines and gets to the point. Speech is quick-fire and incisive. These individuals much prefer action to deliberation, and they are brilliant at simply getting things done with no messing around. They thrive on immediacy and other people's ineptitude or prevarication can drive them crazy.

The downside is impatience, snap decisions that are not properly thought out, or difficulty with entering into debate. "Oh, you mean there are other opinions?" Even if they listen politely, they tend to drive down the "my way or no way" street. Their instant solution-finding nature is a godsend in a crisis but not so hot in the arena of personal relationships. A client with a partner with this Mercury stated that the biggest problem was listening to him having his say but then finding it impossible to have her own. He always went first and once he had got things off his own chest he simply assumed that the "conversation" was over. Nothing was ever properly resolved and the relationship ended, to his mystification and her relief.

IN A NUTSHELL **opinionated, direct, witty.**

MERCURY IN TAURUS

Mercury in Venus' feminine sign communicates carefully. Individuals with this placing often have a story about some kind of restriction in their upbringing that is linked to finding their own voice. Battling shyness or body-image issues, feeling like a misfit, over-protective or unimaginative parenting are all possible factors. For one client it was the lonely experience of being sent to boarding school in a foreign country, which necessitated her having to "learn to speak" all over again. At worst, there is muteness, born of the need for or family practice of ignoring emotional issues or the "seen but not heard" type of childhood.

TAURUS

In spite of early difficulties, however, they generally adopt a common-sense approach to life. Maturity brings charm and they are more likely to play down a drama than to exaggerate it. They are good at finding their niche and resist that which makes them feel unsafe. Barbra Streisand (b. April 24, 1942) is well known for her security fears, stage fright, and the use of a teleprompter to overcome the terror of forgetting words. Mercury in Taurus likes to see things in black and white.

As Taurus rules the throat, the beautiful or earthy voice is also a common feature. Along with Streisand, we find Bono (b. May 10, 1960), Kelly Clarkson (b. April 24, 1982), Bonnie Tyler (b. June 8, 1951), and Stevie Wonder (b. May 13, 1950) all with this Mercury. Speaking voices are just as distinctive, with rich, sexy, full-bodied tones that you would recognize blindfolded, including Morgan Freeman (b. June 1, 1937), Katharine Hepburn (May 12, 1907–June 29, 2003), Orson Welles (May 6, 1915–October 10, 1985), and Laurence Olivier (May 22, 1907–July 11, 1985).

IN A NUTSHELL **stoical, pragmatic, tactful.**

MERCURY IN GEMINI DIGNITY

Mercury and the air sign of Gemini rule everything to do with communication and the function of the mind. The talk-talk planet in the sign of the Twins is therefore the perfect double act. This Mercury loves nothing better than to talk, and speech is quick, animated, amusing, and often excitable. Here we find the hyperactive nature, or the ultimate butterfly mind, effortlessly hopping from subject to subject, or the socially skilled person who can talk to anyone about anything. Skill with language can also show in being bilingual, like Heidi Klum (b. June 1, 1973), whose Mercury is one of five personal planets in this sign, or even multilingual. Sometimes there is a fickleness, but this is often in response to being controlled. This Mercury thrives on diversity and, like air itself, needs to circulate.

Talent with the written word is also a feature, and this placing is extremely common in the horoscopes of novelists, journalists, or prolific songwriters, such as Paul McCartney (b. June 18, 1942) and Billy Joel (b. May 9, 1949). Arguably the most famous diary in the world was written by Anne Frank (June 12, 1929–March 1945), with the Sun and Mercury conjunct (strengthened by sitting next to each other) in Gemini. Ian Fleming (May 28, 1908–August 12, 1964) is also a Sun Gemini, along with Mercury conjunct Pluto, planet of mystery and the underworld, and found fame through his creation of 007 secret agent James Bond.

IN A NUTSHELL **vivacious, clever, creative.**

MERCURY IN CANCER

Mercury in the Moon's sign is usually something of a closed book. This is a water sign, known for being introspective, cautious, and indirect. The mode of expression, even when outwardly extrovert, entertaining, and in full flow, actually gives away very little. These individuals tend to hold their own counsel or will confide only in very close friends, family, or those whose discretion is beyond question. As with the Sun in this sign, the crab shell is a suit of armor, designed to hide vulnerability and to provide a safe haven of withdrawal, and there is usually an intense dislike or even seemingly irrational fear of any kind of confrontation.

This Mercury will go around in circles for an extraordinarily long time before daring to get to the point. Often they never do. Their need for emotional privacy or to protect the status quo can all too easily outweigh the need to voice their true opinions, especially to all and sundry. In the words of one of my Mercury-in-Cancer clients, "Sometimes it's better just to know in your own heart that you are right, without having to prove it. I've learned the value of letting others think what they like."

The real strength of this Mercury lies in the ability to care and counsel. They have a rare talent for true listening without interjecting with their own story. The flip side is a tendency to cling to grievances, old beliefs, to resist change—"It's just the way I am"—or to be overly nostalgic.

IN A NUTSHELL **secretive, evasive, compassionate.**

MERCURY IN LEO

Mercury in the Sun's sign is bold, bright, and self-assured. Speech is firm, clear, and sometimes loud. These people have something to say, they are hard to miss, and the bigger the audience, the better. Here we find extrovert and highly expressive performers, such as Mick Jagger (b. July 26, 1943), Robin Williams (July 21, 1951–August 11, 2014), and Jennifer Lopez (b. July 24, 1969). Yes, they are show offs, but the world needs show offs, either for their entertainment skills or for their ability to put across a message that is aimed at the collective, but which strikes at the heart of every individual. This is the archetype of the speech-maker, those who command respectful attention and make public speaking an art form, for example Barack Obama (b. August 4, 1961) and Nelson Mandela (July 18, 1918–December 5, 2013). Even when the inner nature is humble, they know how to capture a crowd. These people have big ideas and want others to feel their passion; look at Richard Branson (b. July 18, 1950).

What's the downside? Leo's link to royalty and self-importance signals that this Mercury can be pompous, brilliant at making statements and announcements, but not always so skilled at the heart-to-heart stuff of personal relationships. They have to learn that it is not a partner's job to take up the role of audience. Pride or fear of ridicule can also make it hard for them to climb down and admit to being wrong. They secretly, or not so secretly, crave praise and validation. Being appreciated brings out the best in this Mercury sign and when they love you, their adoration knows no bounds.

IN A NUTSHELL **charismatic, demanding, persuasive.**

MERCURY IN VIRGO DIGNITY AND EXALTATION

Most people associate Mercury with Gemini, his masculine sign, but here is his lesser-known strength, the feminine earth sign of diligent Virgo. The planet of the mind in the sign of discrimination makes for an awesome combination—insightful, precise, and observant. These individuals put two and two together and always make four. If something does not add up, they want to know why and they will not rest until they find out. They would never be so brash as to ask direct or impertinent questions, but the polite smile masks a brain that is working at the speed of sound. Nothing escapes their attention, and their power of analysis is second to none.

Speech tends to be measured, economical—why use fifty words when you can

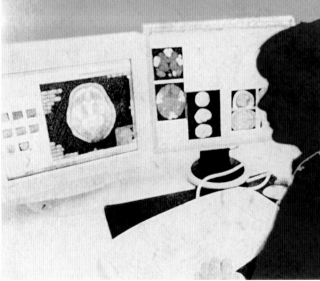

VIRGO

use five—but not necessarily slow. Yes, these Mercury people can be pedantic, nit-picking perfectionists, and guilty of snap judgments, but there is also a quick understanding. Typically, these individuals are highly articulate and deeply interested in the finer details. This is a wonderful placing for a serious novelist or researcher.

The link to Virgo's domain of health also often shows in vocation. One of my Mercury-in-Virgo clients is a top speech therapist. The work goes far beyond diagnosing and treating the actual speech problems themselves, extending into analyzing the family dynamics and having the tact and professional acumen to reveal where a child's verbal difficulties are nearly always linked to their parenting and environment. It is symbolic perfection to see how this is captured by Mercury-in-Virgo Colin Firth in the movie *The King's Speech*.

IN A NUTSHELL **critical, incisive, accurate.**

MERCURY IN LIBRA

The communication planet in the air sign of the Scales speaks in measured, mellow, and often beautiful tones. Here is the born talker and, for that reason, they do not do well being alone. Give the Mercury-in-Libra person someone to talk to, rather than to talk at, and they are happy. Whether it is chewing the cud over cups of tea or glasses of wine, or debating important issues, they can talk for the world. Time slips away and they are not best known for their punctuality.

This Mercury carefully weighs up words and thoughts, so at best this is the diplomat, brilliant at seeing all sides to an issue and appreciating everyone's point of view. They loathe confrontation and are the ultimate smoothers and soothers. At worst, it is the hopeless procrastinator: "I'll think about it, I need to mull it over, I'll do it later, tomorrow, what do you think I should do?"—and on and on. Libra is known for indecision and, with Mercury in this sign, reaching the point of understanding or action can be a tortuous and confusing process, driving themselves and their loved ones nuts in the process. In the words of one client, "It's not making the decision that's the problem, it's sticking to it. I am constantly changing my mind."

Only when they have made a decision that they are able to stick to, or when a decision is made for them, can they be at peace—until the next dilemma.

IN A NUTSHELL **conciliatory, passive, sociable.**

MERCURY IN SCORPIO

Mercury in Mars' feminine sign of intense and secretive Scorpio is, as with the opposite sign of Taurus, associated with silence. Early experiences often carry the hallmark of repression in which speaking freely is disallowed, discouraged, or

SCORPIO

frightening. These individuals are incredibly deep-thinking but have to learn how to communicate authentically rather than clam up or resort to the classic sting-in-the-tail type of sarcasm. They can be overly critical or controlling of others until they learn to subject their own nature and behavior to the same scrutiny. Self-awareness is vital for this placing.

How we do or do not speak about Scorpio's taboo subjects, with sex at the top of the list, is Mercury's domain. Meg Ryan (b. November 19, 1961) did as much for women's sexuality as she did for her own career with the legendary faking an orgasm scene in *When Harry met Sally.* Only a Mercury-in-Scorpio gal could do that justice. Writing about sex is also perfect symbolism for this Mercury. One of my clients has made her fortune by writing steamy books for the Mills and Boon Black Lace series.

With Scorpio's link to both healing and death, this Mercury is the "talking cure," the archetype for the sex therapist, bereavement counselor, and all types of psychoanalysis. The theme of muteness is still in evidence.

A therapist attends to what is not being said, and interprets the coded language of dreams in order to dredge up the precious silt from the teeming riverbed of the unconscious. Mediums and psychics are found here, too, the conduits between this world and another.

IN A NUTSHELL **reserved, bewitching, insightful.**

MERCURY IN SAGITTARIUS
DETRIMENT

In traditional astrology, Mercury is the planet of the so-called "lower mind," which rules our early learning and concerns itself with the minutiae of the smaller picture. Mercury in Jupiter's signs—planet of the so-called "higher mind," which rules adult learning, our philosophy, and the bigger picture—is therefore something of a mismatch. Mercury's voice in fiery Sagittarius is fast, enthusiastic, exuberant, and speaks as it finds. These individuals therefore have a reputation for tactlessness, the classic foot-in-mouth disease, but they don't mean it. The idea of biting their tongue is alien to them, but so is being deliberately hurtful. They learn to tone it down when they realize that others find them overwhelming or even insulting. They also often find it hard to explain themselves and struggle with putting their feelings into words if put on the spot. With time, however, this Mercury placing can be extremely deep thinking, eloquent, and scholarly. This is French writer, historian, and philosopher Voltaire's Mercury (November 21, 1694–May 30, 1778), who was known for his advocacy of freedom of religion and expression. Beliefs run deep, but generally the attitude is cheerful and optimistic rather than overly serious. There is also often an aptitude for learning foreign languages.

SAGITTARIUS

Being honest to a fault is part of their truth-freak nature. Honesty and justice are exceptionally important issues, and they cannot bear to be disbelieved. In terms of indignant reaction, this Mercury can do 0 to 60 faster than any other. If you want to test this, just accuse them of lying—preferably from a safe distance.

IN A NUTSHELL **forthright, visionary, intellectual.**

MERCURY IN CAPRICORN

Mercury expressed through Saturn's feminine sign is controlled, authoritative, and understated. The speaking voice can be rather monotone, although not without resonance, such as the husky tones of Marlene Dietrich (December 27, 1901–May 6, 1992). However, if these individuals ever get really excited about anything you would be forgiven for not noticing. This Mercury does not wear its heart on its sleeve. Guardedness can take the form of quiet reserve, answers that are not really answers, or deadpan humor, all of which are effective deflectors against too much intimacy.

In extremis, this Mercury can put up the "No Entry" sign and close down. If they do not want to talk about something, no amount of pleading, threats, or unashamed begging will make the slightest difference. Only when they are ready to talk do you have a hope of finding out what the problem is, as one of my clients found out the hard way. Her Mercury-in-Capricorn son did not talk to her for nearly five years. When he re-established contact, it was without explanation other than he had had his "reasons."

On a good day, however, these individuals are delightful companions. They may take life too seriously, but that includes the relationships and issues that are important to them. Here we find weighty authors such as Charles Dickens (February 7, 1812–June 9, 1870), or respected actors who take on serious roles, for example Ben Kingsley (b. December 31, 1943). The ultimate Mercury in earthy and structured Capricorn must be Louis Braille (January 4, 1809–January 6, 1852), whose invention of converting sight into touch, today simply known as Braille, has given the gift of written language to countless blind and visually impaired people.

IN A NUTSHELL **courteous, strict, constructive.**

MERCURY IN AQUARIUS

There is a line of thought in modern astrology that considers Aquarius as Mercury's sign of exaltation, although traditional astrology gives this as Virgo. Either way, Mercury expressed through Saturn's masculine sign is a powerful placing. Innovative Uranus as co-ruler, and Aquarius belonging to air—element of the mind—adds up to individuals of above-average intelligence or who have an unusual take on life. Here are the lateral and original thinkers of the zodiac, the types who take to spreadsheets like a duck to water or who can do the Rubik's cube. They have brains like top-speed computers and whoever coined the phrase "thinking outside of the box" must have had this Mercury.

If this Mercury has a problematic side, it usually shows within the arena of personal relationships. Too much head and not enough heart can make this Mercury dispassionate, aloof, or dismissive. Even if they start their sentences with, "I may be wrong but…" they secretly believe that they are right. If you want to convince them otherwise, then make sure you have your arguments at the ready, with all the facts and figures at your fingertips. Sentiment has little place in their world of objective

reasoning and emotional scenes can leave them indifferent or distinctly uncomfortable.

Usually the saving grace with these Mercury people is that they are interesting—and interested. They thrive on conversation and debate, relishing any opportunity to discuss their views or ideas, and love it when you can grab their attention with yours in return. Often they are controversial and admire the same quality of "being different" in others. Chelsea Handler (b. February 25, 1975), with this Mercury powerfully placed on her Ascendant, rose to fame on the strength of wit, humor, writing, television interviewing, hosting, and commentary—all in her own, distinctive and irreverent style.

IN A NUTSHELL **matter of fact, methodical, quirky.**

MERCURY IN PISCES
DETRIMENT AND FALL

AQUARIUS

Mercury in Jupiter's feminine sign can be a fish out of water. We all know what it is like to try and "reason" with someone "in love." Like oil and water, the two simply do not mix. With Neptune, god of the sea, as co-ruler, this Mercury is at the mercy of feelings and thoughts that are free flowing, boundless, staggeringly deep, and teeming with undercurrents. These individuals often have early experiences of emotional hardship, in which their feelings were disregarded or minimalized.

Making sense of emotional matters may be a tall order, but this struggle often produces exceptional poets, singers, and songwriters. What they cannot say as easily or as deeply as they would wish, they express through rhyme and song. The pure voice of Céline Dion (b. March 30, 1968) can be located in her Mercury-in-Pisces exactly conjunct beautifying Venus. Elizabeth Barrett Browning (March 6, 1806–June 29, 1861), with a stellium (four planets or more) in Pisces, including Mercury, penned "How Do I Love Thee," one of the most famous love poems in the world.

The tricky side to this detrimented Mercury is distortion of the truth, from white lies to outright deception. Jeffrey Archer (b. April 15, 1940), with the double whammy of Mercury in Pisces opposite Neptune, is a textbook example. Here is the weaver of tales, the consummate storyteller, the man whose books have sold 250 million copies worldwide, but whose political career was blighted by scandal, eventually leading to imprisonment for perjury. When is it "right" and when is it "wrong" to smudge the line between fact and fantasy? It is all about appropriateness. In a work of fiction, it is a gift; in a courtroom, it is a criminal offence with dire consequences.

IN A NUTSHELL **vulnerable, emotional, empathic.**

VENUS

SIGNS OF DIGNITY: TAURUS AND LIBRA
COLOR: GREEN
DAY OF THE WEEK: FRIDAY
METAL: COPPER

VENUS
Herbs and Foods

Anything sweet, delectable, and more-ish. Chocolate is definitely Venusian, and many Venus types have a sweet tooth. Venus' produce is fragrant or delicious, such as jasmine, apple blossom, all roses, and all soft fruits. Venus also rules thyme, lavender, geranium, vanilla, and any herbs that calm over-indulgence in food.

Venus is Aphrodite, goddess of love, and known as the lesser benefic. Your Venus sign tells you about your relating skills, what you are looking for, and how you approach relationships. She is feminine and rules women, all pleasure seeking, lovemaking, beauty, art, music, and the fashion industry. She also rules sustenance, everything from food to the money we make in order to live.

In a man's chart, regardless of sexual orientation, she often describes the kind of partner he attracts or to whom he is attracted.

VENUS IN ARIES DETRIMENT

Venus is in dignity in Libra, sign of partnership, and therefore is said to be in detriment in the opposite sign of independent Aries. This does not mean that all Venus-in-Aries individuals are doomed to failure in romance, but their task is not an easy one. Ruled by Mars, they are feisty, egotistical, and have strong opinions. They have to learn that partnership needs consultation and negotiation.

Venus people often experienced a troubled adolescence in which they lacked healthy role models and learned to fend for themselves, which in turn tends to arrest the development of relating skills. One of my clients, born with the Sun, Venus, and Mars all in this sign, blazes with vitality and never stops working, having learned early that success in life was down to her. She admires people who risk their vulnerability to find love but says, "I am not willing to do that. And I can't compromise either!"

They may go through long periods of being single, but when they do set out to find a mate, they waste no time. If they like you, there is no mistaking it—they will head straight for you every time they see you. However, they need fast results or they will just move on to their next conquest.

IN A NUTSHELL: **direct, impulsive, impatient.**

VENUS IN TAURUS DIGNITY

Venus in feminine, earthy Taurus is soft, sensual, and tactile. These Venus people thrive on physical contact, although they do have to feel comfortable with you first. This is a safety-conscious sign, but, with emotional security in place, this Venus placing wins hands down when it comes to kisses and cuddles. Princess Diana was famous for many things, but with Venus in her 5th house (the section of the horoscope in which we locate children) her hands-on, affectionate parenting was probably at the top of the list.

These Venus people tend not to rush into love unless they are young. The older they get, the more they deliberate, and the more they will choose reliability and solvency—they love retail therapy—over physical attraction. The flip side to this Venus is complacency. They would be the first to admit to a lazy streak and dislike of change. They may either miss or ignore the early warning signs of love trouble.

As with Mercury in Taurus, the sign that rules the throat, this Venus often denotes the beautiful voice. The "Godfather of Soul" James Brown (May 3, 1933–December 25, 2006), "Slowhand" Eric Clapton (b. March 30, 1945), and Paul McCartney (b. June 18, 1942) all have this Venus.

IN A NUTSHELL: **affectionate, possessive, charming.**

VENUS IN GEMINI

Venus in Mercury's masculine sign is sociable, talkative, and breezy. Their feelings can change rapidly, not through insincerity, but because their boredom threshold is low, so they can also be flighty or sometimes just downright fickle. As Gemini is the sign of the Twins, they are quite capable of having two relationships simultaneously. They are the arch flirters and like to keep their options open, inevitably giving out mixed messages in the process. Understanding their own needs and sexuality can sometimes lie at the heart of contradictory behavior. One of my Venus-Gemini clients put this most aptly when he said that, in some ways, he had the most fun in the days when "I didn't know if I was Arthur or Martha."

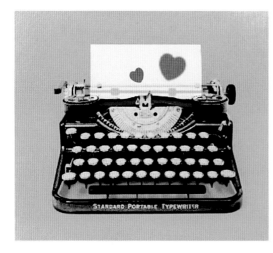

Eventually, however, sexual or commitment issues usually get resolved, choices are made, and this Venus placing indicates at least two major relationships in the course of a lifetime. Tom Hanks (b. July 9, 1956) embodies this Venus perfectly, with his quick and animated style, and two marriages with two children from each. In terms of how Venus symbolizes that which brings us pleasure, and Gemini being the sign of language and communication, Hanks's top hobby is said to be the avid collecting of manual typewriters.

These Venus people need someone to talk to. In love, they make playful and imaginative partners as long as heart and head are both engaged. They are best suited to someone who is intelligent, quick witted, and who knows how to keep them on their toes.

IN A NUTSHELL: **mercurial, amusing, amiable.**

VENUS IN CANCER

Venus in the Moon's sign is caring, nurturing, and fiercely protective towards loved ones. Nobody is allowed to criticize their family except for them, and even then they do so rarely and guiltily. This Venus has a dutiful and filial streak a mile wide and, even if their own family origins were not close, they will usually create one that is. In relationships they are primarily drawn to those who are homemakers, providers, and who want children, but, as with the Sun in this sign, it is a complete myth that this is a given across the board. Sometimes these Venus people can be so fused with their own family that they seem to need no other. Many of them remain single, diverting their care into other outlets, such as their work, home, charity, and close friendships.

This Venus is self-protective, cautious, and often shy, so it is rare for them to get hooked into anything destructive. They are turned on by gentleness, charm, and a sympathetic nature. Loudness or aggression is a big turn off. They are also born romantics and wonderful at looking after you, although the women, in particular, need to guard against becoming "mother" instead of "lover." Similarly with children, a tendency to cling can turn "mother love" all too easily into "smother love." One of my clients could only admit and accept this after both her daughters emigrated to Italy. Needy behavior, never throwing anything away, and saving money—even when they do not need to—are their security blankets, but what these Venus people really need is to be cocooned in love.

IN A NUTSHELL: **loyal, dependable, appreciative.**

VENUS IN LEO

Venus in the Sun's sign is big-hearted, warm, and vibrant. These individuals are usually incredibly generous in the giving of love, and their appetite for receiving it is even bigger. They aim to impress, and a diet of attention, admiration, and adoration is an inexhaustible feast for this Venus. Being told that they are special and wonderful are messages that they cannot hear often enough. When mature and secure, even if they privately yearn for more themselves, these Venus people will dish out the same glorious validation to others, too. However, rejection or embarrassment is their biggest dread, so they usually will not show their own feelings until they are sure of yours. They are also unlikely to seek a mate who is "beneath" them. This Venus can be haughty and wants someone to be proud of.

Actress Mira Sorvino (b. September 28, 1967) shot to fame after winning the Academy Award for best supporting actress for her role in Woody Allen's *Mighty Aphrodite*, stunning symbolism for Venus at 29 degrees of Leo, the degree of the royal fixed star of Regulus. Also known as the Heart of the Lion, Regulus denotes ambition, honor, success, status, and leadership.

LEO

As mentioned in the Moon-in-Leo section, Pippa Middleton has the Moon conjunct Regulus. She also has Venus in Leo conjunct her Ascendant, the angle that rules the physical body. In her figure-hugging Alexander McQueen creation and with perfect poise and straight-backed posture—Leo rules the spine—she all but outshone the bride at the royal wedding.

Suffragette Emmeline Pankhurst (July 15, 1858–June 14, 1928) embodied this lionhearted Venus in another way, through the bravery of her lifelong campaign for the enfranchisement of women.

IN A NUTSHELL: **regal, passionate, demonstrative.**

VENUS IN VIRGO FALL

Virgo's analysis and precision reach their full potential through Mercury, planet of the mind, but these same qualities can be passion killers for Venus. After all, what lover, partner, friend, or child wants to feel as if they are constantly being scrutinized, dissected under a microscope, and given marks out of ten? Whether they are thinking it or saying it out loud, these Venus people tend to have a running commentary in terms of picking apart their loved ones' behavior, habits, views, choices, and so on. However, criticism is rarely the conscious intention. Venus in

Mercury's sign has to understand those they care and worry about, but their challenge is to practice tolerance.

Venus in her sign of fall suggests that these individuals, by definition, should all be celibates, sexually repressed, or not blessed with beauty. This textbook interpretation falls straight into the astrological trap of putting two and two together and making five. Sex symbols with this Venus are plentiful, including Julia Roberts (b. October 28, 1967), Brigitte Bardot (b. September 28, 1934), and Kim Kardashian (b. October 21, 1980) amongst the women, and Patrick Swayze (August 18, 1952–September 14, 2009), Jason Statham (b. July 26, 1967), and John Mayer (b. October 16, 1977) amongst the men. I rest my case.

Venus in Virgo, then, oozes a particular brand of sex appeal. The look is well groomed, beautifully assembled, and never garish. The nature is similarly self-contained and flirting is not overt. They have their own definite partner criteria, usually including good health and a strong work ethic, and discreetly put newcomers to the test. Their reputation for frugality is debatable. Their wardrobe may be minimalist or stuffed with designer labels, some never worn, still with price tags on.

IN A NUTSHELL: **choosy, curious, subtle.**

VENUS IN LIBRA DIGNITY

Venus teaches us all about relating, and she is therefore powerful in the sign of the Scales, the symbol of partnership. There is absolutely nothing that one half can do without affecting the other. These Venus people simply need their other half to be

LIBRA

there, they are inextricably linked, and make heaven-sent partners although they can tip over into too much neediness. They have conventional ideas about togetherness so, unsurprisingly, affairs or long-distance relationships have a short shelf life. They admire beauty and sophistication, and more often than not their partner is a good looker, but ultimately they seek someone who is easy going, relaxing to be with, and equally invested in "The Relationship". One of my Libra-Venus clients has been with the same partner for over forty years, they never married or had children, but they run a highly successful business in home decor. They are together 24/7 and suffer no claustrophobia.

Even this dignified Venus, however, suffers from the notorious Libran balancing act of indecision. In the words of a client:

SCORPIO

"I often stand at crossroads—can I be a mother and still have my career, can I travel and still be in a relationship—all choices are difficult because they always involve someone else."

In terms of aesthetic values, this Venus tops the bill. My favorite anecdote is from a client who told me that, in his seriously broke days, he once spent his last five pounds on a bunch of flowers, on the basis that they would cheer him up and last a lot longer than food.

IN A NUTSHELL: **attentive, artistic, compliant.**

VENUS IN SCORPIO DETRIMENT

Venus in Mars's feminine sign is intense and deeply emotional, although you would be forgiven for not thinking so on first impression. These Venus people do not wear their hearts on their sleeves, to put it mildly. Co-ruled by Pluto, there is a secretive streak and a need to stay in control of their feelings. This belies a passionate nature, and they may even come across as cold or indifferent. Often there is some disturbing experience in their childhood or adolescent life that taught them to give away nothing. Abuse stories are tragically common. Having suffered from powerlessness, they instinctively or consciously protect their vulnerability and nobody gets through the security gates without careful screening.

These Venus individuals usually ooze sex appeal, mystery, and look drop-dead gorgeous in black. They admire strength and bravery and need a partner who is bold and gutsy. Passivity bores them. They know all about the power of sex but are prone to jealousy or possessiveness. However, when secure or truly put to the test, they make awesome partners. Their all-or-nothing nature means that they can do "for better, for worse, in sickness and in health, until death do us part" better than anyone. Former First Lady Hillary Rodham Clinton (b. October 26, 1947) survived the sex scandals of her husband and went on to excel in her own political career. She is especially known for encouraging the empowerment of women on a global scale.

Venus in Scorpio has a highly developed sixth sense and can also symbolize the psychic or the healer.

IN A NUTSHELL: **impervious, powerful, alluring.**

VENUS IN SAGITTARIUS

Venus in Jupiter's masculine sign is a free spirit and an open book. What you see is what you get. They do not play games, and they get confused, impatient, or bored with those who do. When they give their heart away, which they do easily and enthusiastically, their loyalty, fidelity, and total belief in their loved ones follow automatically. In this respect there is a naivety with this Venus. These individuals often go through all kinds of romantic experiences and their share of crushing disappointments before learning that love does, at least sometimes, need common sense as well as faith. When unhappy, they can be prone to promiscuity and disastrous affairs, but generally their innate optimism enables them to bounce back and move on. Of all the Venus signs, this is probably the least likely to end up embittered.

SAGITTARIUS

Freedom is a big issue. These Venus people do not equate needing space with a lack of commitment and being with a partner who wants to be joined at the hip is usually a claustrophobic disaster. Clinging vines need not apply. They can do unconventional relationships as long as the trust is there. They also need an intellectual equal, someone who loves to exchange ideas and philosophize. A partner with good financial skills helps, too, as their own approach to money and all things practical can be rather unrealistic, especially in their younger years.

Being attracted to someone from another culture as a life partner, especially in the case of men, is a common occurrence for this Venus. As an example, British singer David Bowie's (b. January 8, 1947) first wife Angie was American, his second wife Iman is Somalian.

IN A NUTSHELL: **honest, trusting, unrestrained.**

VENUS IN CAPRICORN

Venus in Saturn's feminine sign takes all affairs of the heart seriously. These "get real" individuals generally seek a partner who is hard working, who cares about material security, and who will be there for the long haul. Even in their younger years innate caution, often springing from a strict or restricted upbringing, keeps them from jumping into any relationship too quickly. True commitment is a big responsibility and a big deal.

These Venus people are known for their endurance, sense of responsibility, and pragmatism. They are perfectly capable of passionate attractions, but the choice of a life partner can be treated with the same sang-froid as the choice of a house, car, or job. The first person I ever knew who found her marriage partner through the Internet had this Venus. I am going back over 20 years, to the days when this activity still raised eyebrows, but this anecdote is picture perfect for illustrating how finding love was an important project. She had definite criteria, especially in relation to children and parenting capabilities, and wanted a partner who was solvent, serious, and responsible. She found him, and it worked.

As so often with this sign, there are stories of a curtailed childhood, so these individuals can sometimes seem aloof or older than their years. They usually learn early on about restraint, respectfulness, and duty. This is King Felipe VI of Spain's Venus (b. January 30, 1968), who ascended the throne in June 2014 at the age of 46, making him the youngest monarch in Europe. Capricorn rules structure and tradition, so this Venus also symbolizes the necessity for a "professional" partner who will take his or her place in the hierarchy.

IN A NUTSHELL: **steadfast, formal, assiduous.**

VENUS IN AQUARIUS

Venus in Saturn's masculine sign is an enigma. As discussed in Chapter One, there is a double-sided nature to Aquarius that can essentially be described as the conventional (Saturn) versus the unconventional (Uranus). This split also shows when expressed through the other planets and, in my view, especially through Venus. Here we come up against the strait-laced, repressed, or asexual nature, or the person who is into wild experimentation and up for anything. Both types struggle with connecting with their authentic feelings and often find it hard to express themselves with passion, even when they privately feel very strongly.

The most successful relationships for these Venus people are those that spring from friendship and a meeting of minds. They admire brains and ideas and are especially drawn to a mate who shares both their intellectual interests and their social scene. Unhappiness is usually the result of overriding compatibility issues. They are quick to recover from disappointment, however, and tend to keep ex-partners as friends.

With the Aquarian's concern with the collective, these Venus individuals can do a lot of good when they swing their searchlight out into the world. Oprah Winfrey (b. January 29, 1954) has the Sun and Venus almost exactly conjunct with each other in this sign. This Venus is also a hallmark of the political woman, Christine Lagarde (b. January 1, 1956), for example—the French lawyer, former finance minister (the first woman to hold this post for a G8 country), and current head of the International Monetary Fund (IMF). In true Aquarian spirit, Lagarde believes that the institution is more important than the rise of any individual.

IN A NUTSHELL: **broadminded, unusual, convivial.**

VENUS IN PISCES EXALTATION

Venus in Jupiter's feminine sign is compassionate, empathic, and imaginative. In many ways, these individuals are the ultimate romantics, and they can be blissfully happy if they are lucky enough to find their soul mate. However, they are also extremely vulnerable and, more usually, the quest for love brings a much higher than average rollercoaster of emotional highs and lows. As with the Sun in this sign, their feelings are easily crushed, and the art of self-protection does not come readily. Co-ruled by Neptune, their feelings can be positively oceanic and personal boundaries are a struggle. They are driven by the urge to merge but are secretive when insecure. Escapism can blossom into phenomenal creative achievement when it is channeled into the arts, but the other extreme is to anaesthetize pain through alcohol or drugs. Both Heath Ledger (April 4, 1979–January 22, 2008) and Kurt Cobain (February 20, 1967–April 5, 1994) had this Venus.

Empathy entwined with a self-sacrificing streak also picks out this Venus as an archetype of the rescuer; they are a pushover for a sob story or the longing to be rescued. The two are often confused. In love, these Venus people fare best with partners who are kind yet not over-indulgent and who have their own strong sense of self.

In a man's chart, in particular, this Venus often speaks of his relationship with "the feminine" on a broad spectrum. Either he is at ease with his own feeling self, with a marked preference for female company, or his emotional nature is walled off and projected onto the "over-sensitive" women in his life.

IN A NUTSHELL: **idealistic, gentle, receptive.**

MARS

SIGNS OF DIGNITY: ARIES AND SCORPIO

COLOR: RED

DAY OF THE WEEK: TUESDAY

METAL: IRON

MARS
Herbs and Foods

All that is sharp, stinging, pungent, hot, and spicy, including garlic, ginger, onion, nettles, thistles, horseradish, pepper, paprika, and cayenne. Rocket, considered to be an aphrodisiac, also belongs to Mars.

In traditional astrology, Venus is feminine and rules women, Mars is masculine and rules men. Together they are the love planets, Venus in terms of pleasure and relating skills, Mars in terms of pursuit, lust, and libido. Mars in a woman's chart, regardless of sexual orientation, often describes the kind of partner she attracts or to whom she is attracted.

Mars is the god of war and symbolizes everything to do with how we go into battle and how we handle the cut and thrust of life. Psychologically, he symbolizes heated emotions and he rules anger, passion, and pain.

MARS IN ARIES DIGNITY

Mars in the dynamic and positive fire sign of Aries is just where he wants to be. "No messing," "get it sorted," "do it now," "cut to the chase"—such are the mantras for these speedy individuals. Their sense of immediacy and urgency is second to none, and they are the least likely people to put things off. Similarly, they are usually at the front of the queue when help is needed, particularly for the underdog. With their ability to cut through red tape and pull all the right strings, fearless campaigning is one of the hallmarks of this winning combination. Human rights are especially close to their hearts.

Mars in Aries is proactive (plans ahead) as opposed to reactive (deals with it when it happens). These guys spend their lives on high alert, constantly anticipating all possible scenarios, troubleshooting, and working out a plan of attack. They are fiercely independent, do not suffer fools gladly, and can channel anger into their beliefs.

Love is boring unless it is a challenge. This Mars thrives on the thrill of the chase and needs a partner who can keep their attention.

IN A NUTSHELL: **egotistical, immediate, proactive.**

MARS IN TAURUS DETRIMENT

Taurus is slow and sensual, comfortably at home with Venus, but can punch and bellow when expressed through Mars. Actors who embody this Mars in their work include Robert de Niro (b. August 17, 1943), who played the boxer in *Raging Bull*, and Bruce Willis (b. March 19, 1955), the indestructible hero of the *Die Hard* movies. Alternatively, the Mars-Taurus combination signals inertia, the couch potato, or the nature that is peaceable until provoked. Physically, this Mars has the constitution of an ox but is something of a plodder and hates to be rushed. Results are won through soldiering on, stubborn perseverance, or the "I'll prove you wrong" kind of determination.

This placing is often associated with brutality and bullies. It is the stuff of hard knocks and can signify early experiences of abuse, especially in a woman's chart. Charlize Theron (b. August 7, 1975) was 15 when her mother shot her father. The shooting was ruled as self-defense, the result of years of drunken assaults on both his wife and daughter.

This earthy, masculine streak to Charlize rings out loud and clear in the way she describes herself. She has been quoted as having said that, "I'm 50/50 on glamour stuff. I'd rather put on a pair of jeans and get on my Harley and act like a guy," and manifests in tough roles, such as the leading role in *Monster*, for which she won an Academy Award.

IN A NUTSHELL: **deliberate, blunt, enduring.**

MARS IN GEMINI

If you want to pick a fight with a Mars-Gemini person, you had better have your dictionary at the ready. Mars in Mercury's sign is incisive, quick-witted, and highly articulate. Here are the warlords of words and the masters of verbal volleyball. They fight with their brains. Think civil rights activist Martin Luther King, Jr. (January 15, 1929–April 4, 1968), who received the Nobel Peace Prize in 1964 for his policy of nonviolence. His legendary "I have a dream" speech is regarded as one of the most influential achievements in the history of American oratory. Conversely, words as weapons can show as sarcasm, the throw-away lines of thoughtlessness, wounding intentionally or unintentionally with barbed comments or flippancy, or the hatchet journalist, pursuing any line of enquiry just to get that story.

GEMINI

Mars in the double sign of the Twins can also signal the individual who is multi-talented or who holds down two jobs. They are generally not perfectionists and can make quick work of tasks and to-do lists that others would find time consuming. Typically, they run off nervous energy, have countless ideas, and spend a lot of time on the phone. They can talk anyone into anything or themselves out of any tight corner. Mars in Gemini in O. J. Simpson's (b. July 9, 1947) chart is the significator for his lawyer, the man responsible for his acquittal. As Mars symbolizes men, women often have two significant relationships or marriages, such as Camilla, Duchess of Cornwall (b. July 17, 1947).

IN A NUTSHELL: **quick, inventive, versatile.**

MARS IN CANCER FALL

Note that any Mars-Moon combination is tricky as signaled by their conflicting signs of dignity/exaltation (strength) and detriment/fall (weakness):

- The Moon is dignified in Cancer, Mars's sign of fall, and is in detriment in Capricorn, Mars' sign of exaltation.
- Mars is dignified in Scorpio, the Moon's sign of fall, and is in detriment in Taurus, the Moon's sign of exaltation.

Mars prefers to move in straight lines, but Cancer is depicted by the sideways-moving crab. Mars is direct and pointed, Cancer is cautious, inward looking, and prone to avoidant behavior. They want to be needed, but at the first sign of trouble, pain, or rejection, Mars-in-Cancer individuals will retreat into their shell, keeping hurt inside, or employ passive-aggressive tactics.

Their sensitivity is such that mood swings can happen quickly and with little warning. They also fear giving offence. They will go all around the houses, test the water, and need others to read between the lines.

We could say that there is a hurt child in all of us, but, with Cancer as the sign of family and roots, there is often some notable early damage for these individuals. Amongst my own Mars-in-Cancer clients are sad stories ranging from being separated from their mother at birth to being wrenched away from family life to be sent to boarding school at a tender age.

LEO

IN A NUTSHELL: **moody, protective, indirect.**

MARS IN LEO

Mars in the Sun's sign is a royal, commanding, creative, and powerful combination. These individuals have forceful personalities, and their talents are usually expressed in a center-stage way. Their self-belief is wholehearted, but they need others to believe in them, too. They are highly motivated by praise, recognition, and adulation. The Mars-drive coupled with the Leo-knack for drawing a crowd creates a showmanship quality, charismatic performers, and "the show must go on" work ethic—just think of "The Boss" Bruce Springsteen, (b. September 23, 1949), whose best-known albums have been said to be the epitome of his skill to find the splendor in the struggles of daily life. In business, this is the archetype of the managing director, the Chief Executive Officer (CEO), and the entrepreneur, such as Donald Trump (b. June 14, 1946).

This placing often bestows an excellent physique.

Amongst the women we find statuesque types, such as Charlene, Princess of Monaco (b. January 25, 1978), and supermodels Yasmin Le Bon (b. October 29, 1964) and "The Body" Elle McPherson (b. Match 29, 1964). Amongst the men, think Harrison Ford (b. July 13, 1942) as Han Solo in Star Wars or as the intrepid Indiana Jones.

Leo correlates to the 5th house of the zodiac (see Chapter Three), in which we find children. From my own client work, I have frequently found this placing to denote an adored and usually artistically talented child. Lovers also belong to the 5th, and these Mars people embody the art of courtship.

IN A NUTSHELL: **creative, bossy, bighearted.**

MARS IN VIRGO

Mars in the second of Mercury's signs is the epitome of precision, in word and in action. Here we find the hallmark of the artisan, pure craftsmanship, and the honing of skills. I have seen this placing in the charts of those whose work requires the "cutting edge," such as picture framing or tiling, and in those who have exceptional talents in the worlds of technical drawing, fine art, and intricate design. This Mars is measured, diligent, patient, and painstaking, and the attention to detail is second to none. These guys know how to "sweat the small stuff," a concept that lies at the heart of astronaut Chris Hadfield's (b. August 29, 1959) philosophy and NASA training. Trust me, if you ever decided to travel into space, you would want Colonel Hadfield with his Sun, Venus, and Mars all in Virgo at the controls.

In love matters, this placing can be problematic. The red planet can find it hard to sizzle in Virgo, even though, as noted earlier, Virgo's "prim and proper" reputation is misleading. However, the particular combination of Mars in Virgo can signal issues with sexuality or celibacy. Stephen Fry (b. August 24, 1957), with both Sun and Mars in Virgo, struggled to keep his homosexuality secret during his teenage years at private school, and by his own account did not engage in sexual activity for 16 years from 1979 until 1995.

In my own client work, this placing has frequently shown for those whose happiness is thwarted by the quest for non-existent perfection, for celibates, or for those in platonic yet otherwise functioning marriages.

IN A NUTSHELL: **picky, fastidious, exacting.**

MARS IN LIBRA DETRIMENT

Traditional astrology tells us that Mars is weakened by being in Venus' sign. In basic psychological terms this makes sense, as Mars is the god of war and the go-getter, whereas Libra is the sign of negotiation and peace. There is an obvious conflict, but this does not mean that Mars in Libra is ineffective. On the contrary, the fight (Mars) for peace (Libra) can be a major concern for these individuals, such as it was for John Lennon (October 9, 1940–December 8, 1980), whose iconic songs "Give Peace a Chance" and "Imagine" were both taken up as anti-war anthems.

Mars in Libra is also brilliantly expressed through working (Mars) relationships (Libra). Both William (b. June 21, 1982) and Catherine (b. January 9, 1982), the Duke and Duchess of Cambridge, have Mars in this sign—William at nine degrees and Kate at ten degrees. This reflects their unity as they go about their royal duties. In my own client work I have found that Mars-in-Libra people have a lot of charm but rely heavily on their partner, often to the extent of feeling aimless and unmotivated when having to do things alone or feeling like a failure in their (rare) single periods.

These Mars people are social animals and need others to inspire and encourage them, so they tend to under-achieve if left to their own devices for too long. They generally dislike overt confrontation, although they can be last-word freaks, and tend to cloak anger in distaste.

IN A NUTSHELL: **likeable, dependent, diplomatic.**

MARS IN SCORPIO DIGNITY

As with Mars's other sign of dignity, Aries, the hallmarks of this placing are a competitive streak and determination of the "where there's a will, there's a way" variety. However, whereas fiery Aries tends to blaze a public trail towards personal excellence, the water sign of Scorpio is more undercover. Here is the archetype of the secret agent, the private detective, the sleuth, the psychoanalyst—and the control freak. These individuals have very definite ideas on how things should be done and they do not like to be contradicted or overruled. When feeling threatened or

SCORPIO

insecure, they can invoke the art of the subtle put-down better than anyone, effectively disempowering the competition with a strategically placed sting of the tail. Anger tends to take the shape of inward fuming, and the more serious their rage, the more deadly their revenge.

Mars in Scorpio takes time to fathom. What you see is definitely not necessarily what you get. A calm and dignified exterior, donned especially with new people in new situations, conceals a deep-feeling nature. Underneath the charisma lies a fierce intensity and it is rare for them not to get what they want. Once they learn how to conquer jealousy or control issues, they make amazing partners and, with huge libidos, lovers. They will fight tooth, claw and sting for those they love.

IN A NUTSHELL: **controlling, passionate, insightful.**

MARS IN SAGITTARIUS

Mars in the fire sign of the Archer is bursting with feverish activity. These individuals tend to approach life with tons of enthusiasm but sometimes find it hard to stay focused, often leaving a task or project unfinished when something more interesting beckons. They have restless minds, itchy feet, and need a lot of space. Often their lives are characterized by moves that create the freedom to travel, learn, or explore.

In this respect they are not generally career people, finding it difficult to stay in one job for any length of time, although they are perfectly capable of reaching the top of their tree once they find the right cause. Neither do they enter into committed relationships easily unless they find a true soul mate. In love they need truth, honesty, and a long rein. The paradox is that they are intensely loyal. In their earlier years they may play the field more extensively than anyone, but at heart they are sincere and easily, even naively, bestow faith in those they care about. The women are often well suited to partners of a different ethnic background or culture. In anger, they will flare up in an instant, especially if wrongly accused, and they can be hurtful in the heat of the moment, but never bear a grudge.

Another hallmark of this Mars is equestrian sports, such as polo—Prince Charles (b. November 14, 1948) and Prince Harry (b. September 15, 1984) both have this Mars.

IN A NUTSHELL: **energetic, friendly, faithful.**

MARS IN CAPRICORN EXALTATION

Mars in the earth sign of goal-orientated Capricorn is the embodiment of harnessed energy and unwavering purpose. Here are the empire builders of the zodiac. They are incredibly hard working as they tackle each new project. Their eye is already on the next step upwards, and new challenges just make them work even harder. They thrive on achievement, and their phenomenal staying power usually lies at the root of their success and their drive towards material security.

This placing usually signals a great deal of self-control and restraint, such as being uncomfortable with public displays of emotion or affection. Anger stops short of real fireworks, but the black clouds of a seriously bad mood can linger for a long time. They are not lacking, however, in earthy passion, but this is for behind closed doors. At heart, they are conventional as opposed to emotional risk takers, they value long term, lasting relationships, and they like to know exactly where they stand. Move the goalposts at your peril. Often they choose a partner who is older, especially an authority figure or someone who has already "made it." Catherine Zeta-Jones (b. September 25, 1969) is a textbook example of this Mars, described as "incredibly hard working" by *Chicago* producer, the late Martin Richards, and marrying iconic actor Michael Douglas, exactly 25 years her senior as they share the same birthday.

IN A NUTSHELL: **dedicated, purposeful, traditional.**

MARS IN AQUARIUS

Mars in the fixed air sign of Aquarius signals a nature that is generally smart, competent, and objective. With their systematic approach, they are the ultimate list tickers and can shift enormous amounts of work through being highly organized and logical. Often they make great team players, or they are good at managing teams, as they are masters of the overview rather than being intent on individual glory.

However, although they can see what is best for most, the paradox is that they can be inflexible. Utter personal conviction and high principles can result in a fixed

AQUARIUS

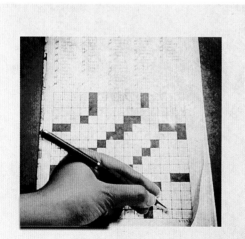

code of ethics from which no one is allowed to deviate. This can create problems when it comes to the give and take of relationships. In love, they can be slow to open up to intimacy and tend to place friendship and shared intellectual interests over passion.

Overall, when it comes to fighting a cause, this Mars is nevertheless in a league of his own. These individuals are also attracted to partners who are similarly strong-minded and on their own mission. Michelle Obama (b. January 17, 1964) and Carla Bruni-Sarkozy (b. December 23, 1967) are both Sun in Capricorn— Saturn's other sign—with Mars in Aquarius.

Steve Irwin (February 22, 1962–September 4, 2006) also had this Mars very powerfully placed in his chart, along with three other planets in Aquarius. Steve was a textbook Pisces in so many ways, but in this cluster of planets in Aquarius, co-ruled by innovative Uranus, we find his "mad professor" streak, the whacky, brilliant guy with an ecological cause.

IN A NUTSHELL: **principled, progressive, original.**

MARS IN PISCES

Mars in the mutable water sign of Pisces creates two contrasting images. Either it is the graceful speed of the beautiful, iridescent fish flashing through the water, or it is the slippery fish, the type that is crafty or amoral. The former approaches life in an imaginative, creative, or romantic way, the latter in a deceptive, manipulative, or fearful way. Here we find the archetype of the con artist, the seducer—this is Giacomo Casanova's Mars (April 2, 1725–June 4, 1798)—or the "poor me" victim who plays, consciously or unconsciously, on the finer feelings or vulnerabilities of others. In my own client work, this Mars has been seen as the "struggling artist," who drained his girlfriend's bank account over a period of years and vanished when the money ran out, and a son in prison on drug charges.

Whether they use their talents for good or ill, these individuals tend to operate on instincts rather than on rationale. At worst, it is others who make the sacrifices, at best, this is a charitable Mars, the self-sacrificing person who will work their fingers to the bone in order to ease the suffering of those truly in need.

Mars in Pisces is a subtle and complex energy. They dread rejection and anger is passive-aggressive, often learned from an early environment in which it was not safe to express strong feelings. Anger can be mistaken for hurt, so these individuals are more likely to cry, sulk, or brood than throw things.

This Mars also often embodies the struggle between awesome creativity and artistic talent, versus the lure of escapism from harsh reality through the means of alcohol or drugs. Johnny Cash (February 26, 1932–September 12, 2003), with the Sun, Mercury, Mars, and Ascendant all in Pisces, faced this battle, as portrayed in the movie *Walk The Line*.

N A NUTSHELL: **hypersensitive, elusive, imaginative.**

JUPITER

SIGNS OF DIGNITY: SAGITTARIUS AND PISCES
COLORS: PURPLE, DEEP BLUES
DAY OF THE WEEK: THURSDAY
METAL: TIN

JUPITER
Herbs and Foods

Jupiter herbs are said to be cheering and benevolent. They include red clover, dandelion, asparagus, and sage. Jupiter also rules fertile soil, grapes, raisins, and wine.

Jupiter is the sixth of the personal planets and thus plays a role in the delineation of personality. However, he is notably slower-moving than the other personal planets, changing sign only once every twelve months. Therefore, in order to individualize this planet further, it helps to consider its house position (the sections of the wheel of the horoscope when divided into 12, see Chapter Three), as well as its sign. Hence, for each chart, there are two Jupiter sections to read:

- Jupiter by sign
- Jupiter by house position, regardless of which sign he is in

For example, if you have Jupiter in Gemini in the 10th house:

- First read Gemini (3rd house) as the primary interpretation
- Then read Capricorn (10th house) for extra insight

In the following snapshots, the qualities may describe the individual's nature and/or may be more recognizable in others, such as family or partners, or in life experiences.

In traditional astrology, Jupiter is known as the greater benefic. His main principle is expansion, and he is the bringer of joy, good fortune, opportunity, higher education, freedom, and travel. He rules all things foreign, both people and places. He is also the planet of truth and humanity, ruling the law, justice, religion, philosophy, and the higher mind. His nature is optimistic, encouraging, and extrovert.

ARIES OR 1ST HOUSE

Positives: unswerving, dynamic, the entrepreneur.
Negatives: superior, overly impulsive or self-serving.

JUPITER IN ARIES OR 1ST HOUSE

Jupiter loves the bigger picture, and Aries is matchless in finding the most direct route from A to B. This combination denotes a trailblazing nature and the visionary. The level of self-belief is notably high, and these Jupiter people rarely stop to think whether something is achievable or not. The gap between thought and execution is minimal, and they aim straight for the target, either for their own desires or in the interest of an important cause. For them, second place is for losers.

TAURUS OR 2ND HOUSE

Positives: dependable, comforting, the provider.
Negatives: sedentary, complacent or the struggle to find inspiration.

JUPITER IN TAURUS OR 2ND HOUSE

Jupiter in Venus' feminine sign is materialistic, appetitive, and enjoys the good life. The means to do so can either come from a wealthy family or through being self-made. This is Aristotle Onassis' Jupiter, powerfully placed in his 2nd house of finances. However, Jupiter's entrepreneurial nature is not always free flowing in this sign of fixed earth. Opportunities can be slow to materialize, or too much family security can kill the hunger that so often characterizes the fulfillment of potential.

JUPITER IN GEMINI DETRIMENT OR 3RD HOUSE

Jupiter is said to be weak in Mercury's signs and vice versa, but this does not denote that Jupiter blessings pass by these individuals. However, they may be hard won. Jupiter rules publishing; Harry Potter was rejected by 12 different publishers until J. K. Rowling found lucky 13. The multiplicity of the Twins also signals a series of books rather than a one-off. In my own client work, this Jupiter has shown as two marriages, both to foreigners, and as the achievement of two degrees.

JUPITER IN CANCER EXALTATION OR 4TH HOUSE

Benefic Jupiter in the Moon's sign is the ultimate protector. These Jupiter people usually have a close relationship with one or both parents. In turn, they often find themselves in a markedly caring role, either in their personal relationships or through their vocation. Sometimes their personal freedom is limited as a result.

Cancer's connection to the homeland can also signify patriotism. The dominant feature of Nelson Mandela's horoscope is this Jupiter conjunct Pluto (power and transformation), encapsulating his life's purpose to challenge white supremacy and win human rights for the South African people.

JUPITER IN LEO OR 5TH HOUSE

Big, bold Jupiter is at his most creative and most obvious in fiery Leo. This combination is all about the confidence and expression of the individual. These Jupiter people generally have tons of personality and considerable "pulling power" through personal magnetism, the ability to command attention, or artistic talent. Often there is the influence of someone who has absolute belief in them. This is Céline Dion's Jupiter, whose then-manager, now-husband, René Angélil, mortgaged his home to fund her first record.

JUPITER IN VIRGO
DETRIMENT OR 6TH HOUSE

Expansive Jupiter in picky Virgo can show in fretting over details, the obsessive-compulsive, or too much work and not enough play. With purist Virgo's link to diet and health, here we also find food intolerance or allergies, the faddy eater, or the teetotaler. This Jupiter is powerful for those who find their vocation in the health industry or whose life purpose is bound up in allegiance to others, often at huge personal cost. This is the Jupiter of Burma's Aung San Suu Kyi

VIRGO

GEMINI DETRIMENT OR 3RD HOUSE

Positives: breezy, playful, and full of ideas.
Negatives: flippancy, skepticism, or "above the law" behavior.

CANCER EXALTATION OR 4TH HOUSE

Positives: loyal, a safe harbor, strong sense of national identity.
Negatives: long-winded, clingy, or over-protective of loved ones.

LEO OR 5TH HOUSE

Positives: devoted, big-hearted, and a sense of occasion.
Negatives: show offs, grandiosity, or the struggle to shine.

VIRGO DETRIMENT OR 6TH HOUSE

Positives: meticulous, discriminating, and efficient.
Negatives: joylessness, servitude, or too many personal sacrifices.

JUPITER IN LIBRA OR 7TH HOUSE

Jupiter in the sign of the Scales is fair, reasonable, and considerate. Here is the original Mr. Nice Guy who finds it easy to be pleasant and impossible to be vindictive. It is rare for them to say a bad word against anyone. This Jupiter acts for the good of the other and is a blessing for all relationships. This is Roger Federer's Jupiter (b. August 8, 1981), who laid out his priorities in advance of the birth of his second set of twins, saying he would not hesitate to miss any tournament to be with wife Mirka. He did just that, pulling out of the Madrid Open Masters.

JUPITER IN SCORPIO OR 8TH HOUSE

Jupiter expands whatever he touches. With Scorpio, that means feelings, the good, and the bad. There are no indifferent ones. These Jupiter people live life intensely and tend to take huge risks, emotionally or in pursuit of a goal. They can be immensely successful when they follow their passion. Sir Cameron Mackintosh (b. October 17, 1946) knew from the age of eight that his future lay in theater production. Emotional spectacles of power, sex, and death, such as in *Les Misérables*, probably the best known of his shows having been seen by 65 million people around the globe, are Jupiter-in-Scorpio personified.

JUPITER IN SAGITTARIUS DIGNITY OR 9TH HOUSE

Jupiter's qualities and concerns resonate with Sagittarius, sign of learning, travel, and exploration of all kinds. These Jupiter people often have a foreign theme of some kind in their lives; they paint on a broad canvas and approach life with enthusiasm, optimism, and a deep sense of trust. They intuitively know that things happen for a reason, which makes for an effective safeguard against bitterness or cynicism. In crisis, they can make a crucial leap of faith and, in doing so, create their own "luck." They are truth freaks with a pronounced sense of right and wrong.

JUPITER IN CAPRICORN FALL OR 10TH HOUSE

Capricorn belongs to Saturn, who symbolizes the opposite principles to Jupiter. This combination is therefore full of conflict and can speak of the struggle between pleasure vs. duty, freedom vs. discipline, or the "for your own good" type of miserable upbringing. At worst, this is a blinkered nature that brooks no disobedience or differentness. At best, this is the workhorse, the ambitious individual who fights against all the odds, such as Charlie Chaplin (April 16, 1889–December 25, 1977), whose childhood was blighted by hardship and the workhouse.

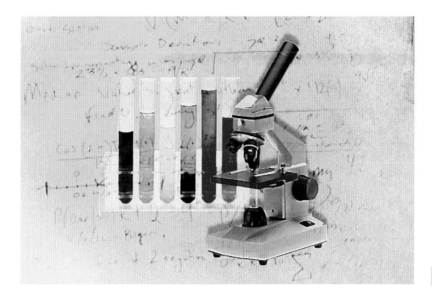

JUPITER IN AQUARIUS OR 11TH HOUSE

Mr. Big—Jupiter in the sign of the collective—sees what is best for most. These Jupiter people are bright, objective, and scientific, approaching life's issues and crossroads with head rather than heart. This is Albert Einstein's (March 14, 1879–April 18, 1955) Jupiter. They like to deal with facts and figures rather than personal agendas, their own or other people's. They make natural leaders, managers, or "breaking the mold" politicians, such as Barack Obama. Often they find their blessings through their friendships or peers.

JUPITER IN PISCES DIGNITY OR 12TH HOUSE

Jupiter's softer concerns, such as care, compassion, and the spiritual life, are beautifully expressed through sensitive Pisces. These Jupiter people have an enormous capacity for love, although, as so often with this sign, the road to happiness is often paved with experiences of suffering or sacrifice. This Jupiter therefore steers many individuals into the caring or artistic professions. Tina Turner (b. November 26, 1939) found her reserves of inner strength and peace through Buddhism, enabling her to escape from the violent marriage to Ike and enjoy a phenomenal professional comeback.

AQUARIUS

AQUARIUS OR 11TH HOUSE

Positives: principled, revolutionary, a social conscience.
Negatives: rigid, dismissive, or the struggle for personal attention.

PISCES DIGNITY OR 12TH HOUSE

Positives: philanthropic, selfless, a connection with the mystical.
Negatives: victims, over-emotional, or the search for meaning.

SATURN

SIGNS OF DIGNITY: CAPRICORN AND AQUARIUS
COLOR: GRAY
DAY OF THE WEEK: SATURDAY
METAL: LEAD

SATURN
Herbs and Foods

The most important Saturn herb is comfrey, which has bone- and skin-healing properties and encourages cell regeneration. Saturn's foods are bitter or sharp, including spinach and parsnip.

ARIES FALL OR 1ST HOUSE

Positives: enterprising, self-belief, the refusal to give up.
Negatives: anger or confidence issues, headstrong, symbolic headaches, or physical migraines.

TAURUS OR 2ND HOUSE

Positives: dependable, constant, the sugar daddy.
Negatives: set in one's ways, stockpiling, money for money's sake.

Saturn is the seventh and last of the personal planets. He still plays a role in portraying character, but he is very slow moving, changing sign only once every two and a half years. The slower the planet, the more it will speak of a backdrop to life rather than just the personal nature. In order to individualize Saturn further, it helps to consider his house position (see Chapter Three) as well as his sign. As for Jupiter, for each chart, there are two Saturn sections to read:
- Saturn by sign
- Saturn by house position, regardless of which sign he is in

For example, if you have Saturn in Libra in the 9th house:
- First read Libra (7th house) as the primary interpretation
- Then read Sagittarius (9th house) for extra insight

In the following snapshots, the qualities may describe the individual's nature and/or may be more recognizable in others, such as family or partners, or in life experiences.

In traditional astrology, Saturn is known as the greater malefic. His main principle is contraction—the opposite to Jupiter's expansion. If Jupiter is "yes," then Saturn is "no." He is the bringer of solemnity, restriction, obstacles, boundaries, endings, and ultimately death. Saturn is the enemy of the "Lights" of life, the Sun and Moon, being in detriment in their signs of dignity, Cancer and Leo. He rules authority, career, duty, and responsibility. His nature is pessimistic, realistic, and serious.

SATURN IN ARIES FALL OR 1ST HOUSE

Aries is fiery, dynamic, and ego-centered, energies that are thwarted when expressed through the solidity of Saturn. These Saturn people invariably experience frustration or intense aloneness in situations of new vs. old, self vs. family, or the individual against the system. Courageous convictions are a hallmark of their missions or identity issues. Chaz Bono (b. March 4, 1969), transgender child of Sonny and Cher, has Venus and Saturn at exactly the same degree in this sign, symbolizing the rejection (Saturn) of his feminine (Venus) self (Aries).

SATURN IN TAURUS OR 2ND HOUSE

Saturn in Venus's feminine sign is mostly down to earth with a "no frills" approach. Here we find astute business types, especially in the fields of finance and produce, such as Linda McCartney (September 24, 1941–April 17, 1998). Responsibility for or attitude to money and security is a major issue. At best, this Saturn is the archetype of the benefactor. Early hardship, however, is not uncommon, either through genuine lack or because financial help is withheld; this can signal a family doctrine of "stand on your own two feet," no matter what.

SATURN IN GEMINI OR 3RD HOUSE

In psychological terms, Saturn is the *Senex* (the wise old man), whereas Mercury, ruler of Gemini, is the *Puer aeternus/Puella aeterna* (the eternal youth). Here we find the old head on young shoulders, or vice versa, but both tend to a youthful outlook. They usually prefer to talk than write, which can be an arduous process, sometimes as a result of difficulties with early schooling. Similarly, a blind spot around paperwork can lie at the root of a general resistance to worldly concerns, such as paying bills on time, if at all.

SATURN IN CANCER DETRIMENT OR 4TH HOUSE

With Cancer's connection to early roots, it is not uncommon for these Saturn people to experience a tough start to life, mostly linked to the struggles or even a tragic history of one or both parents. Drew Barrymore's (b. February 22, 1975) mother was born in a Displaced Persons Camp in Germany, while Drew's own childhood was lost to her parents' divorce, stardom, drug and alcohol abuse, as told in her autobiography *Little Girl Lost*. The transition to adulthood can be a lonely one but often teaches the ability to self-parent.

SATURN IN LEO DETRIMENT OR 5TH HOUSE

Leo is hot and glorifies the individual, Saturn is cold and rules the hierarchy, so this combination is an obvious clash. As in Aries, this combination bears the hallmark of personal limitations vs. the system. This is Bill Clinton's (b. August 19, 1946) Saturn, posited in his 10th house of public life; his efforts to conceal his affair led directly to his impeachment. In my own client work, with Leo's link to children, this Saturn has shown as parental favoritism, but also for a woman who regarded her decision to become a single parent as the best thing she ever did.

SATURN IN VIRGO OR 6TH HOUSE

Saturn resonates with the earth signs, and this combination is industrious, exacting, and disciplined. These Saturn people like to put their resources of brains, time, and money to good use, so they can also be scrupulously frugal. They hate waste, but they are the first to evaluate a job, roll up their shirt-sleeves, and put their shoulder to the wheel. They usually see the details that others miss. Richard Branson's (b. July 18, 1950) Saturn (empire) in Virgo (Virgin brand name) in his 2nd house (money) symbolizes the business that has made him one of the richest men in the world.

GEMINI OR 3RD HOUSE

Positives: information gatherers, constructive, family longevity.
Negatives: head in the clouds, dyslexia, unpunctual.

CANCER DETRIMENT OR 4TH HOUSE

Positives: strong survival instincts, understanding burdens of others, the ancestral home.
Negatives: melancholia, emotional neglect, the broken home.

LEO DETRIMENT OR 5TH HOUSE

Positives: authoritative, choosing personal responsibility, fulfillment later in life.
Negatives: depression, living in another's shadow, skin problems.

VIRGO OR 6TH HOUSE

Positives: conscientious, strong work ethic, the health/business specialist.
Negatives: fear of poverty, the workaholic, obsessive-compulsive behavior.

Positives: a strong marriage, fairness, total commitment.
Negatives: fear of being alone, sitting on the fence, low sense of entitlement.

Positives: fearlessness, phenomenal will power, turning negatives into positives.
Negatives: emotional repression, absolutism, being overly controlled or controlling.

Positives: humanitarian, ethical, barristers and professors.
Negatives: blind faith, cowed by authority, learning difficulties.

SATURN IN LIBRA EXALTATION OR 7TH HOUSE

It makes sense that serious Saturn is exalted in Venus's sign. Relationships are where we are at our most effortful and are the means by which we learn and mature. Many celebrities born under this Saturn are known as much for their partnerships, personal or professional, as they are for their individual fame, such as Prince Rainier III of Monaco (May 31, 1923–April 6, 2005), who was married to Grace Kelly, Sharon Osbourne (b. October 9, 1952), married to Ozzy, and Serena Williams (b. September 26, 1981), whose sister and tennis doubles partner is her sister Venus. This Saturn is also the archetype of authority figures at their best, such as the wise judge or the equal rights employer.

SATURN IN SCORPIO OR 8TH HOUSE

Saturn in the Mars-Pluto sign of fixed water has unparalleled depths of desire, persistence, and resilience. Britain's first female Prime Minister Margaret Thatcher (October 13, 1925–April 8, 2013) had this Saturn sitting on her Scorpio Ascendant (self and public face). She was known as "The Iron Lady" and for her famous words, "The lady's not for turning." These Saturn people rarely deviate from their beliefs or routines, and they can move mountains of work almost without anyone else noticing. Often there is a legacy of emotional hardship.

SATURN IN SAGITTARIUS OR 9TH HOUSE

Saturn in Jupiter's masculine sign presents the conflict of two opposing forces or beliefs. Saturn's nature is to restrict, Jupiter's is to learn and liberate, so here we find the serious philosopher, philanthropist, or freedom campaigner, such as Che Guevara (June 14, 1928–October 9, 1967) and Abraham Lincoln (February 12, 1809–April 15, 1865). These Saturn people have to learn how to do battle with authority in life and how to find the middle ground between claiming their own space vs. their responsibility to others.

SATURN IN CAPRICORN DIGNITY OR 10TH HOUSE

Saturn in his own sign of Capricorn is purposeful but always calculating. These Saturn people generally have an ambitious streak a mile wide but also know the pitfalls of making a fast buck. There is an empire builder in all strong Saturnian types, but this Saturn, in particular, is surprisingly versatile and can turn his hand to anything, whether it is children's entertainment (Walt Disney, December 5, 1901–December 15, 1966), the music industry (Simon Cowell, b. October 7, 1959), international media (Rupert Murdoch, b. March 11, 1931), or running a country (Barack Obama, b. August 4, 1961). The flip side of the coin is rigidity and those who never bend the rules.

SATURN IN AQUARIUS DIGNITY OR 11TH HOUSE

Saturn shares his second sign of dignity with innovative co-ruler Uranus. These Saturn people are therefore either "by the book" operators, or they are challengers of anything outdated. Both types have groundbreaking potential in their areas of interest. Here we find the objective, supremely logical brilliance of the scientists, social reformers, or computer wizards. This is Garry Kasparov's (b. April 13, 1963) Saturn, former World Chess Champion turned political activist. Their weak point is being blinkered by very strong personal opinions or detachment in personal relationships.

SATURN IN PISCES OR 12TH HOUSE

Saturn is the reality planet, whereas Pisces is the sign of romance or escapism. Along with the 12th-house themes of loss or self-undoing, this combination adds up to a painful struggle with the demands of a harsh world. These Saturn people often have to realign their dreams with what is actually possible or get entangled in their own nets. Piscean Nick Leeson (b. February 25, 1967), the former derivatives broker, has Saturn at 29 degrees of Pisces, a fixed star called Scheat, which denotes downfall. His staggering losses on the stock market brought about the collapse of Barings Bank, the UK's oldest investment bank, as portrayed in the movie *Rogue Trader*.

CAPRICORN DIGNITY OR 10TH HOUSE
Positives: able, goal orientated, influential father or male role model.
Negatives: overly conservative, unemotional, lack of spontaneity.

AQUARIUS DIGNITY OR 11TH HOUSE
Positives: systematic, impartial, social conscience.
Negatives: fear of intimacy, the moral high ground, the eccentric or outsider.

PISCES OR 12TH HOUSE
Positives: intense empathy, rescuers of the weak, experiences of redemption.
Negatives: victim role, deception, disillusionment.

URANUS, NEPTUNE, AND PLUTO

URANUS

NEPTUNE

PLUTO

These three planets are known as the "modern" planets, so called because they were unknown to ancient astronomy. Each is a co-ruler of a particular sign and not a substitute for the traditional ruler. They are also known as the Trans-Saturnians—the planets that come after Saturn—or as the generational planets, as they take many years to travel through each sign. With these slower-moving planets, interpretation tends to rest more heavily on the house position (see Chapter Three) and the aspects (see Chapter Four) to the other planets.

Evolutionary events at the time of each planet's discovery reflect their symbolic nature. Similarly, those whose horoscopes are stamped by these outer planets often represent the zeitgeist (the spirit) of their time, bringing the message into the consciousness of the collective and becoming the voice of their generation.

URANUS CO-RULER: AQUARIUS

Uranus was discovered in 1781, coinciding with the French and American revolutions and the industrial revolution in England. He is therefore the planet of rebellion, anarchy, social advancement, ecology, and technology. Both Bill Gates and the late Steve Jobs have strong Uranus-Aquarius features in their horoscopes.

In mythology, Uranus is the sky god and he rules all that comes "out of the blue." He challenges all that Saturn stands for, such as hierarchy and traditional rules, and his nature is innovative, explosive, sudden, unexpected, erratic, or unpredictable.

Typical Uranian types are primarily different. Brilliant, quirky, nervy, eccentric, unstable, a wild child or a genius, a scientist or social misfit, they are always unusual, unconventional, or original in some way.

Uranus is at his most powerful for those individuals who have a Uranian-Aquarian theme to their horoscopes.

TEXTBOOK EXAMPLES

Spike Milligan (April 16, 1918–February 27, 2002), groundbreaking, irreverent comedian and strident campaigner, addressing both domestic violence and environmental issues, who suffered from bipolar disorder throughout his life. The "signature" of his horoscope is an Aquarius Ascendant, Uranus dignified in Aquarius in the 1st house (self/physical body), and in aspect to both the Lights, Sun in Aries and Moon in Gemini.

Philosopher **John Stuart Mill** (May 20, 1806–May 8, 1873) was born on an exact Saturn (tradition)-Uranus (new age) conjunction in Libra (the Scales). He was the first prominent male figure in western moral and political philosophy to address the issue of equality for women in his 1869 essay "The Subjection of Women."

NEPTUNE CO-RULER: PISCES

Neptune was discovered in 1846, coinciding with advancements in photography, film, and pharmaceuticals, notably anesthetics. Gas was replacing oil for lighting, bringing with it streetlights and a night life of brightly lit bars. Neptune is therefore the planet of imagination, illusion, glamour, and escapism, from mysticism to the pain-free world of drugs or alcohol.

In mythology, Neptune is god of the sea, and he rules all things marine. Psychologically, his realm is the boundless watery world of the emotions, ruling fusion, suffering, and sacrifice. His nature is subtle, seductive, addictive, mysterious, magical, or disorientating.

Typical Neptunian types are primarily sensitive. They are often artistic, vulnerable, and acutely receptive to other people's feelings and moods, running the gamut from empathy to paranoia.

Neptune is at his most powerful for those individuals who have a Neptunian-Piscean theme to their horoscopes.

PLUTO CO-RULER: SCORPIO

Pluto was discovered in 1930, coinciding most notably with the discovery of nuclear power and the rise of psychoanalysis through the work of Freud and Jung, among others. Pluto is thus associated with the latent power of either potential annihilation or transformative healing. He also signifies plutocracy, the wielding of power through wealth.

In mythology, Pluto is the god of the underworld, and he rules all that is hidden, invisible, secret, or taboo. Entering into therapy constitutes the exploration of our own underworld, unearthing our buried issues in order to heal. One of his images is the phoenix, the legendary bird of rebirth. His nature is transformative, uncompromising, intense, and extreme.

Typical Plutonic types are primarily powerful. Arguably their strongest gift is that of insight, and many Plutonic types are natural psychologists, sleuths, or healers.

Pluto is at his most powerful for those individuals who have a Plutonic-Scorpio theme to their horoscopes.

TEXTBOOK EXAMPLES

Princess Diana, Sun in Cancer, Neptune in Scorpio, and Chiron in Pisces, all linked to one another and to Pluto (an aspect pattern called a Kite, see Chapter Four). This reflects the woman who captured the imagination of the world, her emotional wounds, and the empathic skills that characterized her charity work.

Elvis Presley (January 8, 1935–August 16, 1977), Sun and Mercury in Capricorn both trine Neptune in Virgo, his sign of detriment, and Moon in Pisces square Chiron. The King was the voice of the 1960s and 1970s, and his tragic death the result of drug abuse.

TEXTBOOK EXAMPLES

Sigmund Freud (May 6, 1856–September 23, 1939), whose horoscope heralds Pluto's therapeutic message with a Scorpio Ascendant and the Sun and Pluto flanking the Descendant—the angle of the "significant other"—in his case the one-to-one relationship with his patients.

Scorpios **Marie Curie** (November 7, 1867–July 4, 1934), born with a Sun-Pluto aspect, and Indira Ghandi (November 19, 1917–October 31, 1984) with a Mars-Pluto aspect, both carried Pluto's masculine power and broke into male-dominated worlds, transforming the way ahead for women of the future.

CHIRON, THE MOON'S NODES, AND THE PART OF FORTUNE

CHIRON

MOON'S NORTH MODE

MOON'S SOUTH MODE

PART OF FORTUNE

CHIRON
POSSIBLE SIGNS OF DIGNITY: SAGITTARIUS OR SCORPIO

Chiron was discovered in 1977, coinciding with the rise of the holistic health industry and the subsequent spiraling awareness of the mind, body, and spirit connection. In terms of astrological tradition, Chiron is but an infant without an official sign of dignity, yet he has already found his way into most Ephemerides, the book of tables that tracks the journeys of all the major planets. Chiron is here to stay.

Melanie Reinhart is a recognized Chiron expert and author of *Chiron and the Healing Journey: An Astrological and Psychological Perspective*. Reinhart originally proposed Chiron as co-ruler of Sagittarius, a symbolically appropriate placing for Chiron the Centaur. She has since proposed that a case could be made for Chiron co-ruling Scorpio, sign of healing and magic, but also suggests that, as Centaurs are creatures without dominion, perhaps we do not necessarily need him to rule any particular sign at all. In her book she explains that his importance lies in how he illuminates issues of awakening, for example, health crises and life-changing experiences, the encounter of guides and teachers, and the recapitulation of previously encountered trauma or insights.

In mythology, Chiron is recognized as the most superior Centaur, standing apart from his unruly brethren. Civilized, knowledgeable, and kind, this skilled physician, teacher, astrologer, and oracle is a fount of ancient wisdom. Ultimately, he is the archetype of the Wounded Healer as, unable to use his healing arts upon himself, Chiron gave up his god-status in order to die and thereby end the eternal agony of a poisoned arrow wound. The full power of his message is captured in his "rebirth," being returned to source and immortalized in the constellation of Centaurus.

Those with Chiron prominently placed in their horoscopes often take up the mission for the collective, notably in the role of mankind's healers or educators whose work is destined to survive them for all time.

THE MOON'S NODES

Every horoscope includes the position of the Moon's Nodes. These are not heavenly bodies but imaginary points at which the Moon cuts across the Ecliptic—the celestial sphere that marks the apparent orbit of the Sun. The Ecliptic takes its name from the fact that eclipses can happen only when the Moon is on or near this line.

You will find the position of the Moon's Nodes in their own column in the Ephemerides. You will find only the North Node listed, as the South Node is always at exactly the opposite point. For example, if you have the North Node at 10 degrees of Aries, your South Node will be at 10 degrees of Libra.

The line of the Nodes is personified as a dragon: The North Node marks the point where the Moon crosses the Ecliptic from south to north, known as *Caput Draconis*—the head of the dragon. The North Node is considered as fortunate and as symbolizing good karma, being where the dragon feeds and gains nourishment.

The South Node marks the point where the Moon crosses the Ecliptic from north to south, known as *Cauda Draconis*—the tail of the dragon. The South Node is considered as unfortunate and as symbolizing bad karma, being where the dragon excretes..

The Sun and the Moon (the Lights) symbolize the eyes of the dragon, and the dragon "eating" the Lights refers to the phenomenon of eclipses.

The Moon's Nodes are at their most powerful when acting as a "testimony" to interpretation, underlining a theme that is already in evidence.

For example, Prince Charles' Moon is positioned at 0 degrees of Taurus in his 10th House (the section of the horoscope in which we locate career/public life). As illustrated in the Moon-in-Taurus section, his exalted Moon symbolizes the influential women in his life, especially his mother the Queen, as the Queen's own Sun marries up with this point, also being at 0 degrees of Taurus. This already powerful picture is reinforced by the fact that Prince Charles' Moon is also conjunct the North Node at 5 degrees of Taurus.

THE PART OF FORTUNE

This is also an imaginary point, which is derived through the mathematical formula of the degree of the Ascendant, plus the degree of the Moon, minus the degree of the Sun. Fortunately, all astrological software does the sums for you. Its name speaks for itself, as it simply picks out a lucky degree in the horoscope and, like the Nodes, often acts as testimony to an astrological theme already in play.

TEXTBOOK EXAMPLES

Bill Gates (b. October 28, 1955) whose gift of technology has revolutionized the face of modern life worldwide, has Uranus opposite Chiron at 0 degrees (powerful new beginnings) of Aquarius.

Alexander Fleming (August 6, 1881– March 11, 1955) had Chiron conjunct greater benefic Jupiter in Taurus, sign of physical matter, in the 11th house of the collective. His discovery of penicillin continues to save millions worldwide.

Steven Spielberg (b. December 18, 1946), whose movies address the deepest human wounds of war, terrorism, the Holocaust, and the slave trade, has the Moon conjunct Chiron in Scorpio.

TEXTBOOK EXAMPLES

Victoria Beckham (April 17, 1974) started her journey to success with the Spice (Mars) Girls—Part of Fortune in Gemini conjunct Mars in Gemini, sign of collaboration and the voice in the 11th house (groups).

Brad Pitt (December 18, 1963), the movie-star pinup—Part of Fortune in Capricorn conjunct Mars in Capricorn (sign of exaltation) in the 1st House (the physical body).

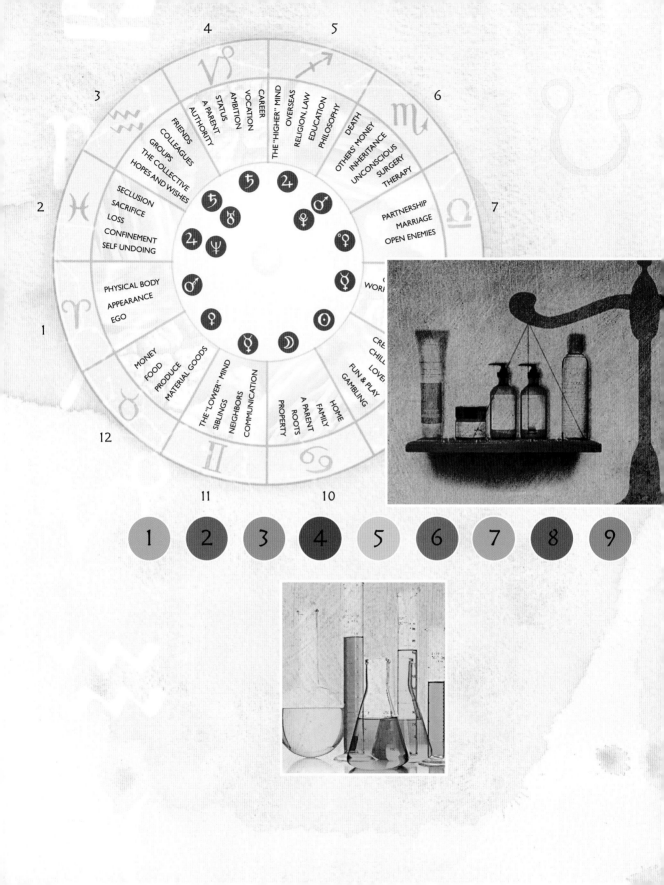

CHAPTER 3

THE HOUSES
AND ASCENDANTS

We start to appreciate the multifaceted depths of
astrology only as we discover how the qualities associated
with the twelve signs of the zodiac adapt and shape
themselves into infinitely variable patterns and possibilities
when expressed through the different natures of the
planets. This kaleidoscope becomes even richer when we
then start to make the leap from general astrology to
horoscopy—the study of individual charts.

Here we find that the wheel of the horoscope is divided
into twelve sections, called the houses, which are a crucial
part of astrological interpretation as they provide the
context for the planets. In other words, when looking at an
actual horoscope, we can immediately see where each
planet "lives." The interpretation of any given planet in
a sign is now further modified and enriched as
we determine its particular role in the life of the
individual or the "native," the person to whom the
natal (birth) chart belongs.

THE HOUSES

The concerns of each house are in keeping with the symbolism of the sign and planet(s) to which they correspond and are numbered anti-clockwise. So, as with the signs and planets, each house has its own dominion, whether this be other people, work matters, health issues, money, and so on.

As we walk through the houses, we venture further into the machinery of the horoscope. Again, and more forcibly, we realize that our chart is not just about "me" in terms of personality, aptitude, or psychological makeup, but it is also about our world and the people, experiences, and concerns that play their roles in shaping our lives. Astrology starts to get very exciting at this stage as we discover that the threads of all our relationships and all our life events are part of the horoscope's rich tapestry.

1ST HOUSE:
ARIES—MARS
The 1st house corresponds purely to the individual in terms of the physical body, appearance, the ego, and sense of self. Here we find the individual at their moment of arrival, prior to any life experience.

The themes of the 1st house reflect the Aries key phrase of "I am."

2ND HOUSE:
TAURUS—VENUS
The 2nd is the house of sustenance, that is, all that is needed for an individual to survive and thrive at a physical level. Here we locate personal money matters, possessions, and material goods. All that can be appreciated through the five senses is located here, including food and all agricultural produce.

The themes of the 2nd house reflect the Taurus key phrase of "I possess."

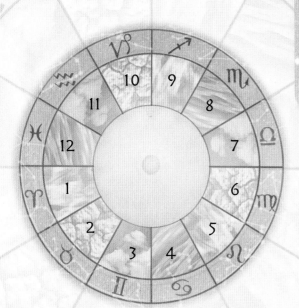

3RD HOUSE:
GEMINI—MERCURY

The 3rd is primarily the house of communication and encompasses everything connected to the written and spoken word—talking, writing, e-mails, letters, the media, phones, computers, conversation, ideas, thoughts, understanding, and so on. In terms of people, the 3rd house rules our siblings and neighbors. It is also our neighborhood, and it rules short-distance travel and all modes of local transport, such as cars, bikes, and buses. Traditional astrology calls this the house of "the lower mind" as it rules early education and mental development.

The themes of the 3rd house reflect the Gemini key phrase of "I speak."

5TH HOUSE:
LEO—THE SUN

The 5th is the "fun house"—parties, hobbies, relaxation, holidays, and anything enjoyable. This encompasses the extremes of hedonism, gambling, and risk taking. It is also the house of creativity, artistic flair, and all that we give life to. In terms of people, children belong to the 5th, those whom we create, and so do lovers, those with whom we share pure pleasure rather than serious commitment or the tougher demands of our world.

The themes of the 5th house reflect the Leo key phrase of "I create."

4TH HOUSE:
CANCER—THE MOON

Here we locate our home and family, where we live now but also our roots, origins, and the environment of our early upbringing. All property concerns belong here. In terms of people, the 4th house rules one of the parents but, even though the Moon and Cancer are more associated with the mother, traditional astrology does in fact give the 4th to the father. In reality, this varies from chart to chart, so the 4th can be either parent. Whether it is mother or father becomes apparent in the study of each individual horoscope.

The themes of the 4th house reflect the Cancer key phrase of "I secure."

6TH HOUSE:
VIRGO—MERCURY

The 6th is the house of work, from menial day-to-day jobs and chores to the expertise of crafts and skills. Health is also located here and all those who work in the health industry. This extends to all areas of service to others, so, in terms of people, servants, skilled labor, or anyone in our employ belong here. Those who serve their country are included in this category, too, so the 6th is also the house of the armed forces. Lodgers are located here, as are pets and all small animals.

The themes of the 6th house reflect the Virgo key phrase of "I serve."

7TH HOUSE:
LIBRA—VENUS

Here we start to find meaning through the rule of opposites. The 1st is the individual, so the 7th is the house of partnership and "the significant other," your other half, marriage, and all major, one-to-one relationships at either a personal or business level belong here. Traditional astrology also says that open enemies or opponents—anyone publicly against you— are to be located in this house.

The themes of the 7th house reflect the Libra key phrase of "I relate."

9TH HOUSE:
SAGITTARIUS—JUPITER

The 3rd represents early learning, so the 9th is traditionally known as the house of "the higher mind." Higher education, philosophy, the search for meaning, religion, truth, justice, and the law, as well as all those who work in these fields belong here, such as teachers, gurus, priests, or anyone who bestows wisdom and gives guidance. The 3rd is our neighborhood, so the 9th is the rest of the world, all things foreign, and those from overseas, the freedom of movement, long-distance travel, and means of transport, especially planes. Publishing and serious literature also belong to this house.

The themes of the 9th house reflect the Sagittarius key phrase of "I seek."

8TH HOUSE:
SCORPIO—MARS AND PLUTO

The 2nd house signifies personal means, so the 8th is the dominion of other people's money and resources, especially the partner's. This is also the house of death and goods of the deceased, which is why legacies and bequests are also found here. The 8th rules sex in terms of the whole cycle of conception, birth, and decay, and also symbolic death, rebirth, and transformation. It is also the house of surgery and surgeons. This is an important house psychologically, as it rules the unconscious and all that is hidden or taboo. The 2nd is the house of the sensual and visible, the 8th is the house of the invisible and the sixth sense.

The themes of the 8th house reflect the Scorpio key phrase of "I regenerate."

10TH HOUSE:
CAPRICORN—SATURN

The 4th represents our home and origins, so in the 10th we locate our place out in the world, our ambitions and aspirations, our public life, profession, and status, where we are going as opposed to where we come from. In terms of people, the other parent is located here, often the breadwinner as opposed to the homemaker, as are all those who have authority over us, from bosses to monarchs.

The themes of the 10th house reflect the Capricorn key phrase of "I master."

11TH HOUSE:
AQUARIUS—SATURN AND URANUS

The 5th is the house of individual creativity and intimate relationships, so in the 11th we locate the wider circle of people outside of immediate family or sexual relationships. Friends, colleagues, associates, our peers, and equals with whom we exchange news and views are all found here. Anything that is linked to the collective belongs to this house, from our social life, groups, and societies, to all kinds of organizations, political systems, or humanitarian or environmental bodies such as Amnesty International or Greenpeace. Along with our ideals, social values, and political beliefs, traditional astrology also calls the 11th the house of "hopes and wishes."

The themes of the 11th house reflect the Aquarian key phrase of "I understand."

12TH HOUSE:
PISCES—JUPITER AND NEPTUNE

Arguably the most difficult house, the 12th is traditionally known as the house of blind spots, ambushes, self-undoing, and the "vale of tears." In terms of people, the 12th is the dominion of hidden enemies, those who plot against us, and also those who are lost to us through estrangement or early death. It is the house of sacrifices and seclusion, so places of confinement are located here, such as hospitals or prisons. The most positive expression of this complex house is retreat in the pursuit of inner contemplation, mysticism, and karmic lessons, and those who devote their lives to the spiritual good of others, such as priests or gurus.

The themes of the 12th house reflect the Pisces key phrase of "I redeem."

IN A NUTSHELL

In terms of astrological symmetry, the houses work in pairs of opposites:

1ST HOUSE
the Self
7TH HOUSE
Significant Other

2ND HOUSE
Personal finances, the resources for life
8TH HOUSE
Shared finances; death and goods of the dead

3RD HOUSE
Communication, local environment, and early education for survival
9TH HOUSE
Higher education and wider horizons, for experience and understanding

4TH HOUSE
Home, family, and private life
10TH HOUSE
Purpose and public life

5TH HOUSE
Personal pleasures and creativity, children
11TH HOUSE
Group pleasures and concerns, friends

6TH HOUSE
Physical health, service
12TH HOUSE
Spiritual life, sacrifice

THE QUADRANTS

The houses are also grouped into quadrants:

- The first house of each quadrant is an angular house: 1, 4, 7, and 10—so called because these houses mark the beginning to the four angles, the main axis of the horoscope. They correspond to the cardinal signs. Planets in these houses are at their most visible, active, and potent.
- The second house of each quadrant is a succeedent house: 2, 5, 8, and 11—so called simply because these houses "succeed" or follow on from the angular houses. They correspond to the fixed signs.
- The third house of each quadrant is a cadent house: 3, 6, 9, and 12—so called because cadent means "falling," so they fall away from the main action, and these houses correspond to the mutable signs. Planets in these houses are said to be at their least visible or powerful.

NATURAL HOUSE

Note that if a planet is in its "own" house, that is, where it belongs in the natural astrological pattern, then it is said to be strengthened by being in its natural house. For example, a 1st house Mars, a 2nd house Venus, a 3rd house Mercury, and so on, would all be natural house planets.

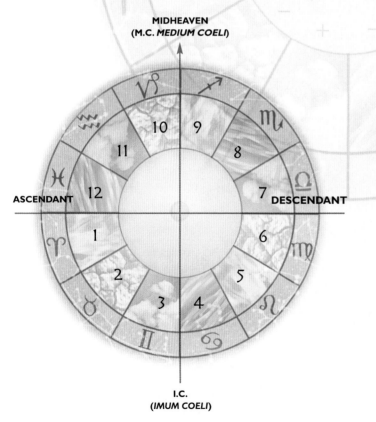

MIDHEAVEN
(M.C. *MEDIUM COELI*)

ASCENDANT

DESCENDANT

I.C.
(*IMUM COELI*)

THE ANGLES

When you draw a line from the beginning of the 1st house to the beginning of the 7th, and then from the beginning of the 4th to the beginning of the 10th, the axis marks the important angles of the chart. The subsequent division of the quadrants creates the trisections of the inner house cusps and the twelve houses. The wheel of the horoscope also acts as a 24-hour clock.

THE ASCENDANT: 6AM OR SUNRISE

Arguably the most important part of the horoscope, the Ascendant—or rising sign—is the sign rising over the eastern horizon at the time of birth. It therefore marks the beginning of the 1st house and is the front door into any horoscope.

THE DESCENDANT: 6PM OR SUNSET

This angle marks the beginning of the 7th house and is always exactly opposite the Ascendant. This is where we locate any significant others in terms of partnership, personal or professional.

THE MIDHEAVEN: MIDDAY

The Midheaven is also known as the M.C., which stands for *Medium coeli*, which is the Latin phrase for the middle of the sky. This angle marks the beginning of the 10th house. In some horoscopes you will find this angle drawn as an arrow, pointing up towards the heavens. The Midheaven points to where we are going, symbolizing our vocation, status, and aspirations in life.

THE I.C.: MIDNIGHT

I.C. stands for *Imum coeli*, which is the Latin phrase for "bottom of the sky," the sky below us. This angle is always exactly opposite the M.C., and it marks the beginning of the 4th house. It symbolizes our origins, where we have come from.

CHART CALCULATION

IS YOUR CHART CORRECT?

The horoscope represents a 24-hour clock and the Sun acts as a marker.

The Sun is nearly always positioned in or next to the house that relates to the time of birth. This can vary slightly in some time zones but even so the sun will be no further than one house either way.

For example, if you have a birth time of 9.00am, the Sun will be in the 11th house (the section of the chart that relates to 08.00–10.00am); if you have a birth time of 9.00pm, the Sun will be in the 5th house (the section of the chart that relates to 8.00–10.00pm).

You may find that this varies slightly when the time falls close to a house "cusp"— the beginning of a house, for example, if you have a birth time of 10.00am, then the Sun will be either in the 10th or 11th house; if it is further away—say in the 9th or the 12th—then you will know instantly that the chart is incorrect.

Learning how to calculate a chart without the use of software is, sadly but unsurprisingly, a dying art. For the serious student there is, in my view, no substitute for pen, paper, and calculator when it comes to a true understanding of the workings of the horoscope, both at a natal and a predictive level. However, there is no denying that computer packages save us hours of work and mathematical headaches. Bear in mind, though, that software is only ever as good as the person using it. It is easy to enter incorrect data, especially in relation to time zones. In order to avoid using a chart that has been generated from incorrect data, here is a quick "look-see" way to check that you have ended up with the right chart:

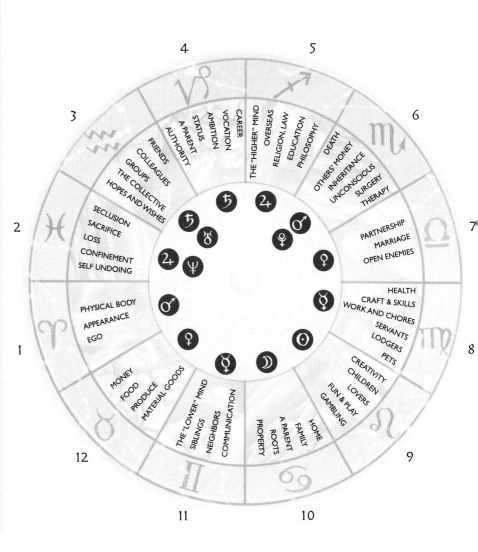

THE ASCENDANT

WHAT IS IT?

The Ascendant (or rising sign) is not a planet but the sign rising over the eastern horizon at the time of our birth; it marks the beginning of the 1st house. This crucial angle can be calculated to exactitude only if the time of birth is known, which is why time is so important to an astrologer. Without a birth time, it is a little like looking at a clock with no hands, so, in essence, the more accurate the birth time, the more accurate the horoscope.

All twelve signs of the zodiac rise over the eastern horizon in any 24-hour period. Owing to a phenomenon called Short Ascension or Long Ascension, some signs pass over the horizon more quickly than others, but as a rule of thumb the Ascendant changes sign approximately every two hours.

WHAT DOES IT SYMBOLIZE?

The Ascendant is the face we present to the world, the personality traits we exhibit and the lens through which we filter all information and experiences. It is the first thing that others see about us or that we see about others. Think of it as the cover of a book. It is not "the whole story" but a flavor of what is to come and an indication of how we come across, how we engage with others, especially in first encounters, and how we approach life in general.

As the angle of the 1st house of the physical body, the Ascendant also has a big say on how we look. As illustrated in Chapter One, all the Sun signs have their own physical characteristics, and these can be replicated when the sign is rising, or when that sign's planet is posited in the 1st house. For example, an Aries Ascendant or Mars in any sign in the 1st house may manifest physically as red hair or sharp features. Physical appearance is summed up as a combination of the characteristics of the Ascendant, Sun sign, Moon sign, and any planet in the 1st house, so the following descriptions will be modified accordingly for each individual.

Similarly, with the Ascendant's link to the physical body, this angle also has to be taken into account for health concerns. Again, these factors originate from the Sun signs and can be replicated through the rising sign.

Regardless of the Sun sign, the ruling planet of any horoscope is the planet that rules the sign on the Ascendant. This planet acts as the native's particular "significator" and is of primary importance in both natal and predictive interpretation. The following descriptions provide an overview of each of the twelve signs when found on the Ascendant. , Note that this information is also relevant when the sign's ruling planet is posited in the 1st house, in any sign. For example, a 1st house Mars shares many of the characteristics associated with an Aries Ascendant.

ARIES ASCENDANT OR MARS IN THE FIRST HOUSE

With an Aries Ascendant, regardless of the Sun sign, the ruling planet of the horoscope is Mars. This planet's sign and house will be a primary consideration in the process of interpretation.

PHYSICAL CHARACTERISTICS Long face and neck, sharply delineated features, often thin-lipped, an aquiline or Roman nose, a pointed or pronounced chin, red hair or red tones to the hair—either natural or added—arched eyebrows, ruddiness in the complexion.

MANNER AND SPEECH Can come across as aggressive, direct, authoritative, or vigorous. The approach to life is generally enthusiastic but impatient, with the focus on action and initiative rather than deliberation. Individuals with this rising sign or a 1st house Mars tend to snap into "how to" solution-finding when faced with a challenge. Language is usually brusque or quick-fire, initially failing to factor in other opinions or practical red lights. Intentions are either self-serving or well-meaning and humane for someone in need of their warrior spirit.

HEALTH Life's demands tend to be handled with powerful bursts of energy, followed by the reaction of exhaustion. Prone to headaches and sinus problems, or injuries to the head or face.

TAURUS ASCENDANT OR VENUS IN THE FIRST HOUSE

With a Taurus Ascendant, regardless of the Sun sign, the ruling planet of the horoscope is Venus. This planet's sign and house will be a primary consideration in the process of interpretation.

PHYSICAL CHARACTERISTICS Strong or jutting chin, square face, neck variable—either short and wide or long and slender, especially in the women—broad shoulders, a muscular frame, a full sensuous mouth, often a concave "ski slope" nose, a gracefulness in movement, even if big-framed or overweight.

MANNER AND SPEECH Can come across as pedantic, deliberate, thoughtful, or seductive. The approach to life is cautious with a tendency to hang back, inwardly running a safety check as an initial response to a new person, problem, or situation. Individuals with this rising sign or 1st house Venus generally resist being coerced into any course of action and can therefore be stubborn, but they know what they want and have particular likes or dislikes. In personal relationships they are the masters of patience, reassurance, humor, and kindness and thrive when receiving the same in return.

HEALTH Usually exceptional stamina. Prone to problems with the throat or thyroid. Often a slow metabolism and a tendency to gain weight easily.

GEMINI ASCENDANT OR MERCURY IN THE FIRST HOUSE

With a Gemini Ascendant, regardless of the Sun sign, the ruling planet of the horoscope is Mercury. This planet's sign and house will be a primary consideration in the process of interpretation.

PHYSICAL CHARACTERISTICS Youthful appearance, fidgety or distinctive mannerisms with the movement of the mouth or hands, small neat features, glittery eyes, usually thin, wiry, or willowy frames.

MANNER AND SPEECH Can come across as nervy, chirpy, flippant, or highly curious. Often, they are animated conversationalists with a childlike sense of fun. Everything is flavored by speed or versatility, whether it is actions, thought processes, or the speaking voice. Individuals with this rising sign or a 1st house Mercury usually have a way with words, including perfect comic or theatrical timing or a quick wit. The flip side is flightiness, a tendency to blow hot and cold, or to mask real feelings behind a jokey "don't get too serious" attitude.

HEALTH A fast metabolism and a tendency to run off nervous energy but bounce back easily from minor ailments. Prone to problems with the respiratory system, the shoulders, arms, or hands, including repetitive strain or other muscular injury.

CANCER ASCENDANT OR THE MOON IN THE FIRST HOUSE

With a Cancer Ascendant, regardless of the Sun sign, the ruling planet of the horoscope is the Moon. This planet's sign and house will be a primary consideration in the process of interpretation.

PHYSICAL CHARACTERISTICS Amiable and mobile features, highly expressive, roundness in the face, "apple" cheeks—sometimes fleshy—full lips, and a wide smile, crinkly or luminous eyes, either large and round or deep set, experts at the sideways glance.

MANNER AND SPEECH Can come across as evasive, ironic, courteous or cautious. As with all the water signs, the approach to new people or situations is somewhat guarded or tentative as they check their findings on an emotional or slightly suspicious barometer. Outwardly, however, this is hard to detect. Individuals with this rising sign or 1st house Moon tend to converse with soft, even tones that express interest and concern, naturally steering the conversation away from themselves and deflecting intimacy until they are ready to drop their guard.

II

Famous Gemini
ASCENDANTS

Reba McEntire, Mick Jagger, Sandra Bullock, Drew Barrymore, Gene Wilder. Kiri Te Kanawa

Famous Cancer
ASCENDANTS

Angelina Jolie, Matt LeBlanc, Cameron Diaz, John Travolta, Judy Garland, Kate Hudson

HEALTH A highly sensitive gut, susceptible to acid stomach or intolerance to particular foods. Prone to inherited genetic conditions or problems in the chest/breast area. The women may also be susceptible to gynecological ailments, especially uterine.

LEO ASCENDANT OR THE SUN IN THE FIRST HOUSE

With a Leo Ascendant, regardless of the Sun sign, the ruling planet of the horoscope is the Sun. This planet's sign and house will be a primary consideration in the process of interpretation.

PHYSICAL CHARACTERISTICS

Well-built and sturdy body, often athletic. The classic leonine look can be even stronger than for those with Sun in Leo, notably the broad face, neat or wide-tipped nose, and the thick or shaggy mane. Excellent posture is also a distinctive feature.

MANNER AND SPEECH Can come across as pompous, warmly welcoming, confident, or commanding. Often they fear ridicule, and they are the experts at assuming a regal manner and putting on a brave face. Individuals with this rising sign or 1st house Sun are also natural organizers or entertainers and have a knack for being at the center of things. They love drama and are quite capable of creating one when life gets too tame, but they are bighearted loyalists and will always rise to the occasion, whether it is a celebration or a crisis.

HEALTH Generally a "love of life" resilient constitution, although prone to back problems or disc injuries. A strong heart but susceptible to cardiac problems in later life unless mindful of a "healthy heart" regime of diet and exercise.

VIRGO ASCENDANT OR MERCURY IN THE FIRST HOUSE

With a Virgo Ascendant, regardless of the Sun sign, the ruling planet of the horoscope is Mercury. This planet's sign and house will be a primary consideration in the process of interpretation.

PHYSICAL CHARACTERISTICS Often a youthful vibe, square head or face, girlish or boyish features that tend to be on the small side but well proportioned, deep-set but lively or questioning eyes, sometimes a prominent forehead.

MANNER AND SPEECH Can come across as superior, critical, inquisitive, or particular. With this rising sign or a 1st house Mercury, everything is put through an analytical sieve until an exact understanding of a person, situation, or task has been reached. They generally take nothing as gospel without checking it out for themselves. They have painstaking patience, superb attention to detail, and a talent for precision in the honing of their skills and crafts, but often set the bar too high in their expectations of others. Meticulous care over personal appearance is also a common characteristic.

HEALTH Health consciousness is usually pronounced, especially in later years. Prone to conditions related to anxiety, intestinal problems, and food allergies.

LIBRA ASCENDANT OR VENUS IN THE FIRST HOUSE

With a Libra Ascendant, regardless of the Sun sign, the ruling planet of the horoscope is Venus. This planet's sign and house will be a primary consideration in the process of interpretation.

PHYSICAL CHARACTERISTICS Often an indication of beauty, symmetrical and softly modeled features, usually a straight nose, a full or well-shaped mouth, sometimes dimples in the chin or cheeks, pleasant and kindly expression, often look younger than their years.

MANNER AND SPEECH Can come across as passive, indifferent, easygoing, or charming. Mostly the nature is extremely amiable, polite, and softly spoken in individuals with this rising sign or a 1st house Venus. Naturals at engaging with others and would rather walk on hot coals than deliberately give offence. In this respect they tend not to air their personal views too soon or too energetically. Similarly, they are the first to placate others and to troubleshoot from a viewpoint of fairness and justice.

HEALTH Physical well-being rests largely on a balanced diet and emotional equilibrium. Prone to kidney problems, diabetes, or vacillating energy, sometimes related to highly sensitive blood sugar levels.

SCORPIO ASCENDANT OR MARS OR PLUTO IN THE FIRST HOUSE

With a Scorpio Ascendant, regardless of the Sun sign, the ruling planet of the horoscope is Mars, with Pluto as the co-ruler. These planets' signs and houses will be a primary consideration in the process of interpretation.

PHYSICAL CHARACTERISTICS Overt or subtle sexiness, chiseled features, beautiful eyes, often with a hypnotic or penetrating "X-ray" quality, frequently a slightly raised bridge to the nose, a brooding expression, and often heavy brows in the men.

MANNER AND SPEECH Can come across as reserved, private, formidable, or fascinating. They have phenomenal reserves of determination and their approach to life and relationships in particular is intense, emotional, and profound. Individuals with this rising sign, and especially a 1st house Pluto, need to forge deep connections and tend to give short shrift to those deemed to be flippant or superficial. New faces and situations are put through remorseless screening and they attach great importance to their first impressions. Usually these are uncannily correct.

HEALTH Mostly resilient with exceptional powers of recuperation from illness or from over-doing things. Prone to problems with the reproductive or excretory systems.

SAGITTARIUS ASCENDANT OR JUPITER IN THE FIRST HOUSE

With a Sagittarius Ascendant, regardless of the Sun sign, the ruling planet of the horoscope is Jupiter. This planet's sign and house will be a primary consideration in the process of interpretation.

PHYSICAL CHARACTERISTICS Tall or big frames, especially the men, large hands and feet, long-limbed, a sporty physique, a swinging stride, and tendency to clumsiness, a prominent and sometimes "horsy" nose, deep-set but quizzical eyes, distinctive laugh.

MANNER AND SPEECH Can come across as friendly, tactless, enthusiastic, or larger than life. Generally there are no hidden agendas and what you see is what you get. Individuals with this rising sign or 1st house Jupiter tend to speak as they find, bestow trust easily, and consequently rarely suspect others of sinister motives. They intuitively put people or situations to the "is this interesting?" test and quickly disengage when bored. The general approach to life is restless, adventurous, freedom-orientated, and optimistic.

HEALTH Generally a fortunate and robust constitution, but need to pace themselves in lifestyle and control the tendency to excess. Prone to problems with the liver and injuries or conditions affecting the hips, thighs, buttocks, or sciatic nerve.

Famous Sagittarius
ASCENDANTS

Hilary Swank, Prince William, Catherine Zeta-Jones, Elton John, Goldie Hawn, Elvis Presley

CAPRICORN ASCENDANT OR SATURN IN THE FIRST HOUSE

With a Capricorn Ascendant, regardless of the Sun sign, the ruling planet of the horoscope is Saturn. This planet's sign and house will be a primary consideration in the process of interpretation.

PHYSICAL CHARACTERISTICS Generally of a large or stolid build, with squareness or distinctive planes to the face. Often striking bone structure, including the cheekbones, and a firm jaw, and prone to ageing gracefully.

MANNER AND SPEECH Can come across as guarded, unsympathetic, gloomy, or proper. In youth they seem older than their years, but younger in their outlook as they grow older. For individuals with this rising sign or 1st house Saturn, life often gets off to a tough start, either in terms of experiencing too much responsibility too soon or by being held back through hardship, oppression, or a rigid family culture, especially through the father. Winning respect and forging self-esteem, ideally through success in their vocation, softens their seriousness or pessimism.

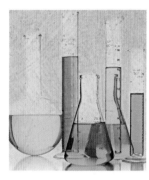

HEALTH Exceptionally hardy constitution and powers of endurance. Prone to difficult-to-treat skin conditions, such as eczema or psoriasis, or aging ailments of bones and joints, especially the knees, such as rheumatism, arthritis, and osteoporosis.

AQUARIUS ASCENDANT OR SATURN OR URANUS IN THE FIRST HOUSE

With an Aquarius Ascendant, regardless of the Sun sign, the ruling planet of the horoscope is Saturn, with Uranus as the co-ruler. These planets' signs and houses will be a primary consideration in the process of interpretation.

PHYSICAL CHARACTERISTICS Saturn types tend to stockiness or heaviness; Uranus types often tend to the opposite due to hyperactivity; piercing wide-set eyes, often a startling blue in fair-skinned types, high forehead, long straight nose, wide mouth, and big smile.

MANNER AND SPEECH Can come across as inquisitive, indifferent, original, or unusual. Individuals with this rising sign, and especially a 1st house Uranus, often have experiences early on in life that set them apart. This, in turn, makes for strong personalities that are very much a law unto themselves. This rising sign also denotes an incisive intelligence but some emotional jet lag, often from a "head-over-heart" upbringing. The initial response to new people or situations is extremely analytical, sometimes giving the impression of distance or coolness.

Famous Capricorn
ASCENDANTS

Queen Elizabeth II, Sean Connery, Marie Curie, Larry King, Sophia Loren, Susan Sarandon

Famous Aquarius
ASCENDANTS

Barack Obama, Whoopi Goldberg, Sylvia Plath, Jay Leno, Roseanne Barr, Jim Morrison

HEALTH Mostly physically robust, although prone to problems with circulation or injuries to the lower leg or ankles. The mind-body connection is particularly important, susceptible to acute depression when "split off" from their authentic selves.

PISCES ASCENDANT OR JUPITER OR NEPTUNE IN THE FIRST HOUSE

With a Pisces Ascendant, regardless of the Sun sign, the ruling planet of the horoscope is Jupiter, with Neptune as the co-ruler. These planets' signs and houses will be a primary consideration in the process of interpretation.

PHYSICAL CHARACTERISTICS

Usually tall or big-boned, face tends to roundness and softness, liquid eyes, generally wide set, sometimes protruding, especially in the men, highly mobile or malleable features, a gentle aura.

MANNER AND SPEECH

Can come across as charming, vague, vulnerable, or compassionate. The approach to life and relationships is extremely tentative or hopelessly idealistic. Individuals with this rising sign, and especially a 1st house Neptune, can be impressionable and suggestible. Often there are early experiences of loss or of being exposed to a harsh reality that leaves them at the mercy of others. They understand suffering and find

themselves through marine, musical, artistic, or altruistic vocations, or lose themselves through escapism or the inability to heal the victim's wounds.

HEALTH A sensitive constitution that needs peace of mind, body, and spirit. When troubled, suffers from insomnia or stress-related illnesses, extremely susceptible to adverse reactions to drugs, alcohol, or anesthesia, prone to problems or injuries to the feet.

HOUSE RULERSHIP

When you first look at a horoscope, one of the first things you will notice is that certain houses are devoid of planets. This does not mean that the houses in question are inactive in any way. An empty 5th house, for example, does not indicate childlessness, just as an empty 7th house does not mean an absence of relationships. Matters pertaining to any house are described in two ways:

- by any planets posited in the house
- primarily by the planet that rules the house

CHART RULER

As already stated, the ruling planet of any horoscope is the planet that rules the sign on the Ascendant. So, if Virgo is rising, the native will be ruled by Mercury; if Libra is rising, they will be ruled by Venus, and so on. When considering the three signs that have a co-ruler (Scorpio, Aquarius, and Pisces), always take the traditional planet as the primary significator and the co-ruler as the secondary. For example, if Pisces is rising, the native will be ruled by Jupiter and secondly by Neptune, the co-ruler.

One of the first vital steps in interpretation is to locate and assess the "condition" of the chart ruler; that is, to determine how strong or weak the planet may be in terms of sign, house, and then aspects (relationship) to the other planets (aspects will be explained in Chapter Four).

HOUSE RULERS

The same scrutiny applies to the ruling planet of each house. For example:

- If we find Sagittarius on the 2nd house cusp, then the native's financial concerns will be described by the condition (sign, house, aspects) of Jupiter.
- If we find Capricorn on the 2nd house cusp, then the native's financial concerns will be described by the condition of Saturn.
- If we find Aries on the 7th house cusp (the Descendant), then the type of partner/the nature of relationships will be described by the condition of Mars.
- If we find Gemini on the 7th house cusp, then the type of partner/the nature of relationships will be described by the condition of Mercury, and so on. Understanding the principle of house rulership is therefore absolutely crucial to the art of chart interpretation. Once you adopt this system, you can locate absolutely anyone or anything in the horoscope. Essentially, this part of astrological craft enables you to ask not just "what is this planet telling me?" in terms of the native's own character and life situation, but also "who is this planet in the native's life?" As above, so below—the planet will describe the concerns of, or the people belonging to, the house in question.

UNDERSTANDING THE VISUAL LAYOUT OF A HOROSCOPE

Let us start with a quick, "back to school" mathematical reminder of the relationship between time and space:

- A clock face contains 360 degrees that are divided into 12 hours. Each hour contains 60 minutes (of time), and each minute contains 60 seconds (of time).
- The wheel of the horoscope contains 360 degrees and, as there are 12 signs of the zodiac, each sign contains 30 degrees. Each degree contains 60 minutes (of space), and each minute contains 60 seconds (of space).

SIZE OF THE HOUSES AND INTERCEPTED SIGNS

There is a variety of "house systems" from which to choose, which means slightly different ways of dividing up the 360 degrees of the horoscope, but the most widely used system is called Placidus. As with most of the house systems, Placidus does not operate on the "equal house" system, which gives exactly 30 degrees to each house. House sizes are variable, every single chart is unique, and the actual size of the houses is determined astronomically by the date, time, and place of birth of the individual.

The houses do not need to be drawn to scale. The circle is simply divided into 12 sections and the number/sign on each house cusp tells you the starting point of each house. The left-hand side and the right-hand side of all horoscopes are always exactly symmetrical—so the 1st house is exactly the same size as the 7th, the 2nd the same as the 8th, and so on.

Occasionally, you will find that some of the individual houses are so big that they take up considerably more than a 30-degree space. This can result in "intercepted signs," whereby one house will include a whole sign that is then flanked by the late degrees of the previous sign and the early degrees of the next.

IN A NUTSHELL—WHO IS WHERE

Each house indicates a relationship of the native (ruler of the 1st house) to others.
Here is a reminder for where to find others in the horoscope:

2ND AND 8TH HOUSES

These houses are not used to locate others. The 8th rules over the dead, the 2nd is the house of possessions, money, and disposable assets.

3RD HOUSE

Brothers/Sisters/Neighbors: Siblings and all taken-for-granted relationships in our immediate environment.

4TH AND 10TH HOUSES

Parents: Parents are indicated by the MC/IC axis, the ancestral time line. Tradition gives the 4th to the father, the 10th to the mother, but this is a variable rule. Those who have authority over us are also shown by the 10th.

5TH HOUSE

Children/Lovers: Those with whom we play, create, and simply enjoy being.

6TH HOUSE

Employees/Servants/Lodgers/Doctors: Those who are unequal to us, who do our bidding and attend us.

7TH HOUSE

Significant Other: Close partners and all important one-to-one relationships—love, marriage, business—as well as open enemies, i.e. those who oppose the native.

9TH HOUSE

Teachers/Lawyers/Priests and Gurus: All those whom we might seek out for help and guidance.

11TH HOUSE

Friends/Peers/Colleagues and Associates: Our wider circle of friends and acquaintances—equals with whom we exchange views. All groups and those to whom we are related by a common interest or social brotherhood.

12TH HOUSE

Secret Enemies/Jailors/Spies: Those who are against us or who confine us, or those who are lost to us.

PRINCE CHARLES'S HOROSCOPE

Regardless of your views on monarchy, working with the horoscopes of royals is helpful practice, firstly because we always have an exact time of birth, and secondly because their lives are conducted in the public eye. Prince Charles's horoscope is an example of intercepted signs. Starting with the Ascendant:

- 1st house starts at 5 degrees of Leo
- 2nd house starts at 22 degrees of Leo
- 3rd house starts at 14 degrees of Virgo
- 4th house starts at 13 degrees of Libra
- 5th house starts at 23 degrees of Scorpio
- 6th house starts at 4 degrees of Capricorn
- Charles's 5th house therefore comprises of 41 degrees:
  - the last 7 degrees of Scorpio
  - the whole 30 degrees of Sagittarius (intercepted)
  - the first 4 degrees of Capricorn
- The 11th house therefore also comprises 41 degrees in the opposite signs, including the whole 30 degrees of Gemini (intercepted).

PRINCE CHARLES

14 NOVEMBER 1948
21:14
LONDON

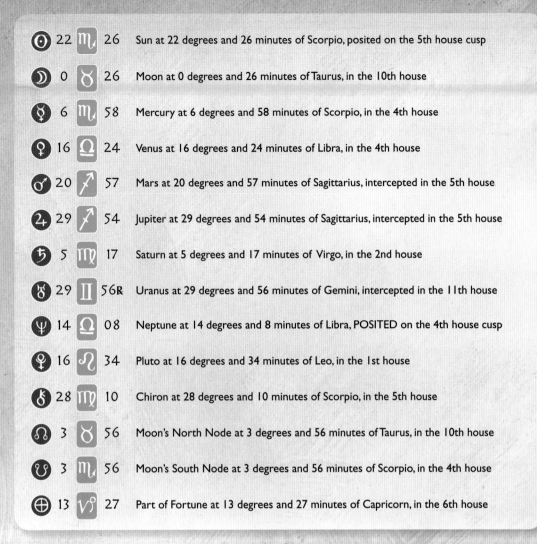

☉	22 ♏	26	Sun at 22 degrees and 26 minutes of Scorpio, posited on the 5th house cusp
☽	0 ♉	26	Moon at 0 degrees and 26 minutes of Taurus, in the 10th house
☿	6 ♏	58	Mercury at 6 degrees and 58 minutes of Scorpio, in the 4th house
♀	16 ♎	24	Venus at 16 degrees and 24 minutes of Libra, in the 4th house
♂	20 ♐	57	Mars at 20 degrees and 57 minutes of Sagittarius, intercepted in the 5th house
♃	29 ♐	54	Jupiter at 29 degrees and 54 minutes of Sagittarius, intercepted in the 5th house
♄	5 ♍	17	Saturn at 5 degrees and 17 minutes of Virgo, in the 2nd house
♅	29 ♊	56ℝ	Uranus at 29 degrees and 56 minutes of Gemini, intercepted in the 11th house
♆	14 ♎	08	Neptune at 14 degrees and 8 minutes of Libra, POSITED on the 4th house cusp
♇	16 ♌	34	Pluto at 16 degrees and 34 minutes of Leo, in the 1st house
⚷	28 ♍	10	Chiron at 28 degrees and 10 minutes of Scorpio, in the 5th house
☊	3 ♉	56	Moon's North Node at 3 degrees and 56 minutes of Taurus, in the 10th house
☋	3 ♏	56	Moon's South Node at 3 degrees and 56 minutes of Scorpio, in the 4th house
⊕	13 ♑	27	Part of Fortune at 13 degrees and 27 minutes of Capricorn, in the 6th house

In regards to house rulership, Prince Charles's chart is a perfect working example in terms of locating his two important relationships:

- He has a Leo Ascendant and is therefore ruled by the Sun, in Scorpio, posited exactly on the 5th house cusp of children and conjunct Chiron. This indicates a healing and educational role through the provision of an heir, rather than being King himself.
- His Descendant is in the opposite sign of Aquarius, traditionally ruled by Saturn and co-ruled by Uranus, two planets with opposite characteristics.
- Serious Saturn, planet of time, obstacles, and delays, sits in patient Virgo in the 2nd, clearly signifying his long-term relationship and later marriage to Camilla.
- Wild-child and rebellious Uranus in his natural house of the 11th—in impish Gemini, sign of the Twins ruling youth and mischief—is a symbolically appropriate significator for Diana, the partner who upset the royal apple cart, who was adored by the collective, and with whom he had two children.

Note
You may not always see the glyph for the South Node actually in the horoscope as it is understood that it is always exactly opposite the North Node. I also tend to write the information for the Nodes and the Part of Fortune without the glyph for the sign, to distinguish them from the planets.

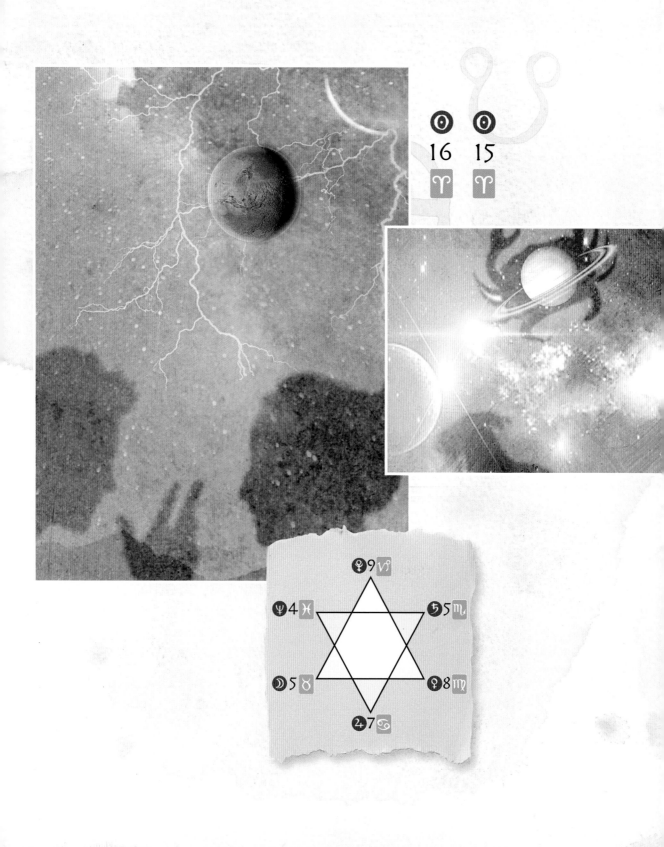

CHAPTER 4
ASPECTS AND CHART INTERPRETATION

Aspects tell us about the relationships between the signs
and, therefore, the planets—whether or not they are
connected, for good or ill, as allies or as enemies.
Harmonious aspects generally reflect our happier
personality traits and the areas of our lives that are
easier and more pleasurable. The inharmonious aspects
reflect the opposite, the troubled parts of our psyche and
the areas of our lives that are characterized by
tension or difficulty. In terms of chart interpretation,
all the major aspects are important in delineating both
character and destiny.

ASPECTS

THE MAJOR ASPECTS

♂
CONJUNCTION

Planets positioned next to each other, 8-degree orb. Harmonious or inharmonious, depending on the planets/signs involved.

☍
OPPOSITION

Planets 180 degrees (six signs) apart, 8-degree orb. This aspect is formed when the two planets are in opposite signs. Inharmonious, the opposition symbolizes conflict or the open challenge to be faced.

△
TRINE

Planets 120 degrees (four signs) apart, 8-degree orb. This aspect is formed when the two planets are in the same element—a strong alliance, positive, helpful, and harmonious.

□
SQUARE

Planets 90 degrees (three signs) apart, 8-degree orb. This aspect is formed when the two planets are in the same mode—at odds with each other, stressful, a source of friction, inharmonious.

✳
SEXTILE

Planets 60 degrees (two signs) apart, 6-degree orb. This aspect is formed when the two planets are both in either feminine or masculine signs— easy, friendly, and harmonious.

There are five major aspects: the first four—the conjunction, opposition, trine, and square—which need an orb of 8 degrees, and the sextile, which needs an orb of 6 degrees. The "orb" means the maximum distance allowed between the two planets for the aspect to be "allowed." When the aspect being made is in orb—allowed—we can then say that the planets in question are conjunct, opposite, square, trine, or sextile each other. For example:

- The Sun at 12♌ and Mars at 16♌ is a Sun-Mars conjunction, as the two planets are less than 8 degrees apart.
- The Sun at 12♌ and Mars at 21♌ is not a conjunction. The planets are in the same sign but they are 9 degrees apart, too wide for the conjunction aspect to count.

Always bear in mind that the tighter the orb, the more powerful the aspect, and therefore the more important it will be.

As introduced in Chapter One, the four elements (fire, earth, air, and water) and the three modes (cardinal, fixed, and mutable) play a vital symbolic role in the delineation of character and life situations, but we now see that they are also crucial at this technical level of locating aspects.

HOW TO SPOT ASPECTS

As well as knowing your elements and modes, it is also helpful to know your polarities—which signs oppose each other—and which are feminine (the earth and water signs) or masculine (the fire and air signs). Having this information as fingertip-knowledge means that you can learn quickly how to spot aspects "at a glance," rather than actually counting the degrees between all of the planets.

THE MINOR ASPECTS

There are several minor aspects, but you most definitely do not need to use the entire list in order to interpret a horoscope. The two that are worth noting, however, are:

⊼

QUINQUNX OR THE INCONJUNCT

Planets 150 degrees (five signs) apart, 2-degree orb. Awkward by name, awkward by nature, as the planets share no element or mode and therefore have no meeting point, for good or ill. It speaks of blind spots, discord, and incompatibility. Inharmonious.

⊻

SEMI-SEXTILE

Planets 30 degrees apart, 2-degree orb—half a sextile, planets in consecutive signs. Variable, depending on the planets/signs involved.

IN A NUTSHELL

Conjunctions are easy to spot as the two planets sit next to each other. Then, as long as the planets are within the given orbs:

PLANETS IN THE SAME ELEMENT

are always four signs apart and therefore trine to each other.

PLANETS IN THE SAME MODE

are either six signs apart—oppositions—or three signs apart—squares.

PLANETS THAT SHARE FEMININE OR MASCULINE SIGNS

are always two signs apart and therefore sextile to each other.

PLANETS THAT ARE FIVE SIGNS APART

or one sign short of an opposition—are quinqunx to each other.

PLANETS THAT ARE ONE SIGN APART

are semi-sextile to each other.

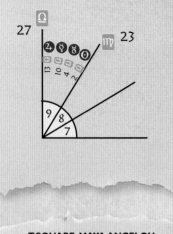

STELLIUM: CATHERINE ZETA-JONES

ASPECT PATTERNS

Aspect patterns are formed when three or more planets are all linked together. As these patterns can be a dominant factor, they can often form the crux of a chart. Note that these patterns are formed only by the planets and do not include the angles of the chart, such as the Ascendant or Midheaven.

STELLIUM

This is like a "daisy chain" of four or more planets making a series of conjunctions in the same sign. (Three planets conjunct each other are called a Triple Conjunction). Often, the first and last planets in the chain are not themselves conjunct, but as long as there are fewer than 8 degrees between each planet, the grouping is a Stellium.

For example, Sun 2 ♎, Uranus 4 ♎, Mercury 10 ♎ and Jupiter 13 ♎ This automatically places a strong focus on one particular sign and on one or more particular houses.

T-SQUARE

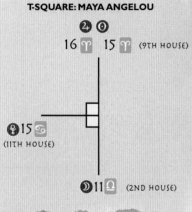

T-SQUARE: MAYA ANGELOU

This is probably the most common of the aspect patterns and is formed by an opposition with both planets making a square to a third. The third planet is often the focal part of the pattern, the "escape route" from the conflict symbolized by the opposition. The T-Square will be more significant if it involves the personal planets or the chart ruler.

THE GRAND CROSS

This is a T-Square with the missing "leg," so it is made up of two oppositions with all four planets in square to the next. Again, note whether the chart ruler or personal planets are involved. This is a stressful aspect pattern, "a cross to bear," especially if in the fixed signs, but it can also denote strength, persistence, and creative talent of the "against all odds" variety.

THE GRAND TRINE

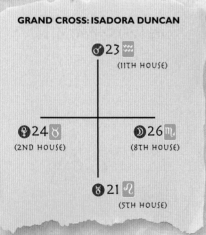

GRAND CROSS: ISADORA DUNCAN

This aspect pattern is formed by three planets forming an equilateral triangle, so look for the presence of all three signs of the same element. This pattern is not as harmonious as you might imagine, as there may be too much emphasis on the one element. Again, consider the condition of the planets and houses involved.

KITE

If you locate a Grand Trine, then look to see if there is an opposition to any of the three planets involved. If the opposing planet then makes sextiles to the other two planets in the Grand Trine, you will have a Kite formation. This aspect pattern can hold considerable power and potential but, in my experience, it also often symbolizes "locked-in" situations that involve ties to others. Note the planets and houses involved and, especially, the condition of the planet making the opposition, the "handle" to the kite, and therefore the focal point of the pattern.

YOD OR FINGER OF FATE/FINGER OF GOD

This is a rare and often painful aspect pattern as it involves two planets in sextile to each other both making a quinqunx, a stressful and "blind spot" aspect, to a third planet. The planet forming the point of this isosceles triangle is the focal point of the pattern.

STAR OF DAVID

An extremely rare aspect pattern, so rare that I have never come across one in my own client work or even in a celebrity chart. Look for two grand trines, six planets all in sextile to each other, creating a Star of David in either masculine or feminine signs. This, presumably, would be a highly fortunate alignment in a natal chart—but this is my hypothetical opinion based on the beauty of the formation and the sympathies between the feminine or masculine elements, and not an empirical interpretation. At the time of writing, the last time this formation happened was on July 29, 2013, in the feminine signs.

Every aspect pattern you locate will be different in terms of the signs, planets, and houses concerned, but the guidelines for assessment are the same:

- Which planet is the strongest—by sign or house?
- Does the pattern include the chart ruler?
- How many of the personal planets (Sun through to Saturn) are involved?
- What is the condition of the focal planet(s)?

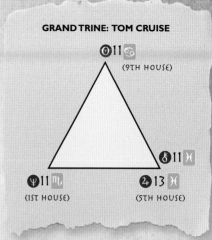

GRAND TRINE: TOM CRUISE

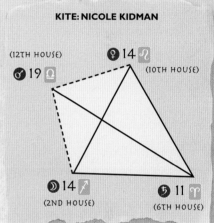

KITE: NICOLE KIDMAN

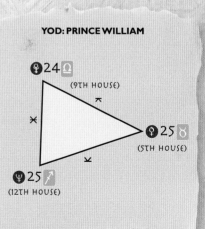

YOD: PRINCE WILLIAM

CHART INTERPRETATION

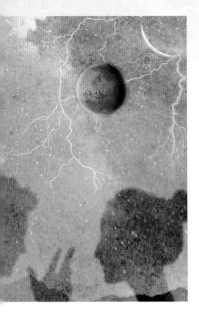

The building blocks of horoscopy follow a logical sequence of signs, planets, houses, and aspects. To familiarize ourselves with the symbolism of the signs, the nature of the planets and their aspects, the meaning of the houses, and the importance of house rulership is to equip ourselves with the tools of the craft needed to make the leap into the world of chart interpretation. In other words, the goal is to start setting the horoscope in motion by converting information into meaning—but where do we start?

Every serious student of astrology, without exception, can reach the point of being technically knowledgeable but will still struggle with the challenge of translating the symbolism so that it "speaks" in an accurate and meaningful way. In many ways we find ourselves learning a foreign language, and just because we have some vocabulary and grammar under our belts does not mean that we can automatically make the leap to fluency.

Absolutely the first principle to remember is that there is a substantial limit on what we can "know" in advance. This is because astrological symbolism work at two levels—the universal and the particular. For example:

- At a universal level, we know that Mars symbolizes our drive, libido, anger issues, and so on. Most astrological literature and websites operate at this level, which is why, when you read a supposed definition of a planet in a sign or any astrological feature, it will more often than not fall short of the "truth."
- At a particular level, Mars will have a far more specific role to play in any given horoscope depending on his "condition"—his position by sign, house, and aspects in relation to the other planets. He will signify other people or issues in the native's life depending on the houses that he rules.

Ultimately, and most importantly, how Mars plays out for any individual can be interpreted only when seen in context. The astrologer's task is to listen to the client's "story" and to locate that story in the symbolism of the chart, as will be demonstrated with Angelina Jolie's chart later on in this chapter.

LOCATING SIGNIFICANCE

Locating significance is a phrase coined by Geoffrey Cornelius and Maggie Hyde, founders of The Company of Astrologers. This is an approach that teaches us how to sidestep the laborious and ultimately pointless exercise of making reams and reams of notes, which may look impressive on paper, but which in reality are usually of little use, especially when face to face with a client. Locating significance simply means finding the meaning by zooming in on what is important in every individual horoscope. It is at this stage that we truly understand the value of knowing our astrological "grammar and vocabulary" and come to appreciate that the art of chart interpretation rests on a bedrock of sound, technical knowledge.

LOCATING SIGNIFICANCE CHECKLIST

By following these guidelines, you can start to unlock the content and possible meaning of any given horoscope.

THE HOROSCOPE VISUAL Most astrologers these days print their horoscopes straight from their computers, drawn up by their software. Call me old-fashioned but, although I use a computer package to do my mathematics for me, I always draw up my charts in my own hand. I strongly advise that you adopt this habit, especially in the early days of study. It is a deeply satisfying ritual at a creative or artistic level and, more importantly, the experience of seeing the chart take shape under your own pen will automatically guide you to what is important. When you have finished drawing up your chart, you will feel an immediate "relationship" with it, something that is harder to achieve when looking at a computer-generated printed chart.

START WITH THE OBVIOUS—THE ANGLES Is there anything yelling for attention, for example, a planet on an angle (the Asc/Desc or the MC/IC)? If a planet is conjunct one of the angles to within 5 degrees, this planet is said to be "angular." The angles are the most visible part of the chart and any planet conjunct them will turn out to be a dominant feature of the chart.

For instance, Bill Gates (b. October 28, 1955) and Tyra Banks (b. December 4, 1973) were both mentioned earlier in the book as they share the placing of their Moon in Aries. Adding the next layer, they both have Cancer Ascendants and therefore are both ruled by the Moon, which, in both horoscopes, is powerfully placed in Aries (initiators, trailblazers) up on the Midheaven (the career angle).

Jennifer Lopez (b. July 24, 1969) is a textbook Leo—and a double one. The Sun at 1 degree of Leo sits exactly on her Ascendant, also at 1 degree of Leo. Born to perform to an adoring public.

Note that if a planet is 5 degrees or less away from an angle when it is marking the cusp to the next house, this planet will belong to this next house. For example, if the Descendant is 10 Libra and the Sun is at 8 Libra, then the Sun would be conjunct the Descendant and would therefore belong to the 7th house and not the 6th.

THE INNER HOUSE CUSPS If a planet is conjunct one of the inner house cusps to within 2 degrees, then this planet is also inviting extra attention, but to a lesser degree than planets on angles. Note that if a planet is 2 degrees or less away from the cusp of the next house, it then belongs to that house. For example, if the 2nd house cusp is 10 Libra and the Sun is at 8 Libra, then the Sun would be conjunct the 2nd house cusp and would belong to this house, not the 1st.

LOCATE THE CHART RULER Assess its condition by sign/house/aspects.

ASPECT PATTERNS Locate any aspect pattern and assess its strength in terms of the planets involved and their condition by sign/house/aspects.

ORBS What are the tightest aspects in the chart? In other words, which aspects are the closest? For example, the Sun at 2♌ and Uranus at 3♌, a conjunction with only a 1-degree orb, will be far more powerful than the Sun at 2♌ and Uranus at 9♌, a conjunction with a 7-degree orb.

PARTILE ASPECTS Partile means absolutely exact, not just to the degree but also to the minute. For example:

The Sun at 5♌30 and Mars at 5♌30 would be a partile conjunction.

Mercury at 2♊35 and Jupiter at 2♈35 would be a partile sextile.

As you can imagine, partile aspects are rare but considered to be very powerful, for good or ill, depending on the planets/signs involved.

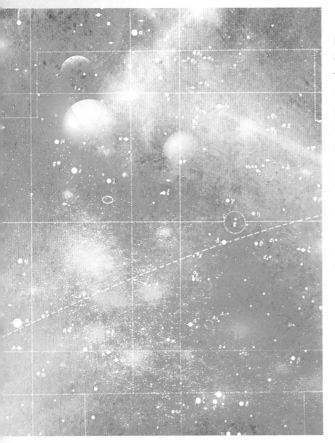

PRIORITIZE As a rule of thumb, consider the personal planets first (Sun through to Saturn), the aspects they make to each other, and then the aspects they make to any of the outer planets (Uranus, Neptune, Pluto, Chiron). Aspects between the outer planets themselves will often be generational, such as Neptune sextile Pluto, which started in the early 1940s and stayed in orb for over fifty years. However, a personal planet sextile to Neptune or Pluto would be particular to the chart and therefore to the native.

UNASPECTED PLANETS Note if there is any planet that stands completely alone, that is, one that does not make any aspects at all to the other planets. This planet will not be integrated into the rest of the chart and will therefore symbolize a specific person/issue that is not integrated into the native's life.

MISSING ELEMENTS Note if there is a missing element amongst the personal planets, Sun to Saturn. This does not mean that the native lacks the qualities associated with the element. It would obviously be nonsense to say, for example, that someone with no water has no feelings. We all have feelings. Rather, a missing element often symbolizes something that was absent, discouraged, or ignored in the person's upbringing, and therefore something that we have to figure out for ourselves. Here are some examples as discovered through my own client work:

NO FIRE
a lack of value placed on spontaneity, risk taking, or the child's individuality, experiences that sabotaged confidence

NO EARTH
a lack of money, physical or emotional security, or lack of instruction regarding survival skills

NO AIR
a lack of encouragement with learning, no interest or value placed on the child's expression of personal views or ideas

NO WATER
a lack of regard for the child's feelings, a family culture of devaluing or suppressing emotions

It is by no means a hard and fast rule, but when you discover an element to be missing, check the Descendant. It is astonishing how often that element is on this important angle as it very often symbolizes what is missing within and therefore what is sought from "the other."

MUTUAL RECEPTIONS This indicates a positive relationship between two planets that occupy each other's signs, even if they are not in aspect. For example, Venus in Sagittarius (Jupiter's sign) and Jupiter in Libra (Venus' sign) would be considered a cooperative partnership. An especially helpful exchange is indicated when the mutual reception involves two planets in detriment/fall but in each other's sign of dignity. For instance, Moon in Capricorn (detriment, but Saturn's sign of dignity) and Saturn in Cancer (fall, but the Moon's sign of dignity). Mutual receptions often signal the option of a move to be made, a "swapping over" from one path to another.

 If you follow this approach to your chart interpretation, you should end up with no more than two pages of notes. This may seem surprisingly meager but remember that, at this stage, you are simply laying the groundwork and preparing the framework for the real interpretation to come.

ANGELINA JOLIE'S HOROSCOPE

Begin by following the guidelines for locating significance in Angelina Jolie's chart.

THE ANGLES

Looking at Angelina Jolie's chart for the first time, you will note immediately, especially if you drew the chart yourself, that there are two planets on angles, Venus in Cancer conjunct the Ascendant and Jupiter in Aries conjunct the Midheaven. Traditional astrology recognizes these two planets as the "benefics." They are both fortunate in nature and indicate many blessings when powerfully placed in the horoscope.

In terms of priority, the Ascendant is the most personal angle of the chart, marking the cusp of the 1st house of the physical body. Venus in any sign conjunct this angle denotes beauty. Venus in Cancer (the Moon's sign) is the perfect symbol for the facial roundness and fullness of Angelina's famous features, and she frequently tops the lists of the world's favorite sex symbols and "most beautiful" women.

Venus is the "outlet" to a cardinal T-Square, being square to the opposition of Uranus and Chiron posited in the parental houses of the 4th and 10th. Note that the Venus–Uranus square part of the pattern has an orb of just 38 minutes of arc

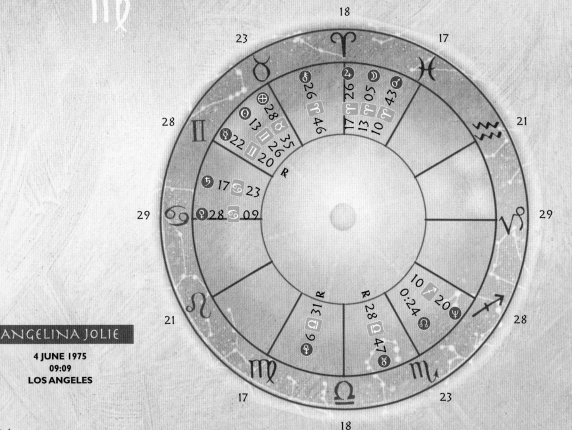

ANGELINA JOLIE

4 JUNE 1975
09:09
LOS ANGELES

Textbook
GEMINI

Coming full circle, it is fascinating to look at Angelina's nature and life story as a Gemini cameo. Gemini's planet Mercury rules all that is mixed or multicolored, a stunning symbolic showing for Angelina's "rainbow" family, three adopted and three biological children with husband Brad Pitt.
Gemini does duality or multiplicity. Fittingly, all the children take the double-barreled name of Jolie-Pitt, and the doubling-up symbolism even extends to her relationship, as Angelina and Brad are known collectively in the media as "Brangelina."

The duality in Angelina's life stretches back much further and, in fact, started at the very beginning, as both her parents were of mixed heritage. She is of Slovak and German descent on her father's side and French-Canadian and Haudenosaunee (Iroquian Indian) on her mother's side.

When you see Angelina being interviewed, you almost forget that she is one of the most beautiful women in the world, as she is open, engaging, animated, and highly articulate. In true Gemini fashion, she laughs easily and gesticulates constantly, often raising her hand to her mouth as the words spill out. Geminis always have a lot to say.

Mercury rules the written as well as the spoken word and Angelina has published her own book about her experiences through her UN work. As a devoted humanitarian, profits from *Notes from My Travels* go to the UN Refugee Agency.

She has also turned her hand to producing and directing, with a documentary called *A Moment in the World*, which in itself is the ultimate Gemini project. She came up with the idea whilst traveling all over the world, moving in and out of different cultures, and witnessing different world events and experiences. She wanted to capture these events simultaneously within a random three-minute time frame, which resulted in gathering over 30 crews and sending them across the world with instructions to start filming at exactly the same time for three minutes.

Gemini individuals love to circulate and to be on the move. For Angelina, that also shows as a love of being airborne. To add to her other Gemini skills, she has achieved a lifelong ambition of getting her pilot's license in 2004.

In this day and age, with soaring divorce rates, multiple relationships are not uncommon for any sign, yet Geminis invariably have at least two marriages or key relationships that play a large role in shaping their lives. Angelina runs true to Gemini type with her two marriages— she was Billy Bob Thornton's fifth wife—prior to meeting and marrying Brad Pitt. She has also openly acknowledged her bisexuality after falling in love with *Foxfire* co-star Jenny Shimizu and says, with her legendary lack of inhibition, that she is surprised that people can still be shocked by the idea of gay relationships.

Even her attitude to money is Geminian, and she divides her income into three parts—one third for her own life and living expenses, one third saved, and one third donated to charity.

(the name for the space between two planets). This reflects the often turbulent relationship with her father, Jon Voight, and also the fact that she is a carrier of the inherited BRCA1 defective gene. Cancer rules the breasts and the uterus, and Angelina lost her mother when she was only 56, her maternal grandmother at age 45, and maternal aunt at age 61 to either breast or ovarian cancer. On diagnosis with the faulty gene, Angelina opted for a double mastectomy to reduce her risk of developing the same disease.

THE CHART RULER

Jupiter in Aries is powerful by virtue of being conjunct the Midheaven, and also because he is part of a triple conjunction in Aries, including the Moon, her chart ruler, and Mars, dignified in his own sign. Jupiter therefore marks the beginning of her 10th house of career and status. The Moon is in the 9th house but is being pulled into the 10th. (At 13 degrees of Aries, the Moon is just within the 5-degree orb of also being conjunct the Midheaven at 18 degrees of Aries.) Mars is in the 9th— house of all things foreign. Note that Jupiter is also sextile to her Mercury, dignified in Gemini. All of these planets reflect her work as Goodwill Ambassador for the UN Refugee Agency and her tireless campaign to promote humanitarian causes worldwide.

Note also that the Moon-Mars conjunction opposes Pluto in Libra in the 3rd (siblings), which may also speak of her reputedly intense relationship with her brother, as well as being part of her own powerful personality. This configuration also symbolizes the depression she suffered in her earlier years, which resulted in collecting knives (Mars) and self harming (Moon as emotional needs and chart ruler) to release her pain.

RULERS OF THE 5TH HOUSE With Scorpio on the cusp of the 5th house, both Mars and Pluto are the significators for Angelina's children. With the Moon (mothering) conjunct Mars in the 9th (foreign countries) and opposite Pluto (loss, transformation), the symbolism fits the adoption of three children who were born into hardship in three different countries—Maddox from Cambodia, Zahara from Ethiopia, and Pax from Vietnam.

In addition to the opposition of the 5th-house rulers, we also find Neptune playing an important role in the configuration. Neptune is posited in the 5th and "mediates" the opposition by being trine the Moon/Mars and sextile to Pluto. Neptune (redemption) is also opposite her Sun in Gemini, sign of the Twins (her first pregnancy produced Gemini daughter Shiloh and the second resulted in her own twins Knox and Vivienne), reinforcing the desire to rescue and create a family. The Moon's North Node at 0 degrees of Scorpio in the 5th and Venus in nurturing Cancer on the Ascendant are both powerful testimonies to the importance of children, and it is not hard to believe her when she says she adores being a parent.

Creativity also belongs to the 5th house, and Neptune aspects are extremely common in those with exceptional acting talents, lending a Piscean flavor and fluidity. Neptune also rules pharmaceuticals and altered states of consciousness, the Sun rules identity and sense of self, and this opposition also manifested as wild experimentation with drugs in her younger years.

DESCENDANT RULER The tightest orb in the chart is the Jupiter square Saturn—just 2 minutes of arc apart. With Capricorn on the Descendant, Saturn is her "significant other," who frequently points to an older partner. Her first marriage was to Johnny Lee Miller (3 years older), the second to Billy Bob Thornton (20 years older), and her third marriage is to Brad Pitt (12 years older).

Brad is a Sagittarian but he has a stellium of four personal planets in Capricorn—Moon, Venus, Mercury, and Mars. He therefore fits the Saturn archetype and, with this planet in Cancer, the sign of family, he also describes the older partner with whom she has children. From a craft point of view, Saturn is Angelina's most difficult planet, being in his sign of fall and with no other aspects other than the square to Jupiter, Moon, and Mars. Also as ruler of the 7th house but posited in the 12th house, he signifies difficult experiences with relationships. We, of course, do not know what goes on behind closed doors, but currently the symbolism accurately reflects the lifestyle of retreating from the world into large guarded houses, restricted freedom, and the constant presence of burly bodyguards.

SATURN AS FATHER SIGNIFICATOR At a universal level, Saturn often signifies the father. Planets in the 12th can signify those who are lost to us, and Angelina has been through several periods of estrangement from her father, including a stretch of six years that eventually ended after her mother's death. Jon Voight fits the symbolism of this 12th-house Saturn perfectly as he himself is a Capricorn with Saturn at 11 degrees of Aries (sign of fall), conjunct his Ascendant at 10 degrees of Aries, which is the same sign and degree as Angelina's Mars, reflecting the anger underlying their conflicts.

MISSING ELEMENTS Angelina has no personal planets in earth, reflecting a start in life that lacked the kind of security that she needed. As suggested earlier, the missing element can often be found on the Descendant, as is the case here, with Capricorn on the 7th-house cusp, indicating that grounding would come through the right partner.

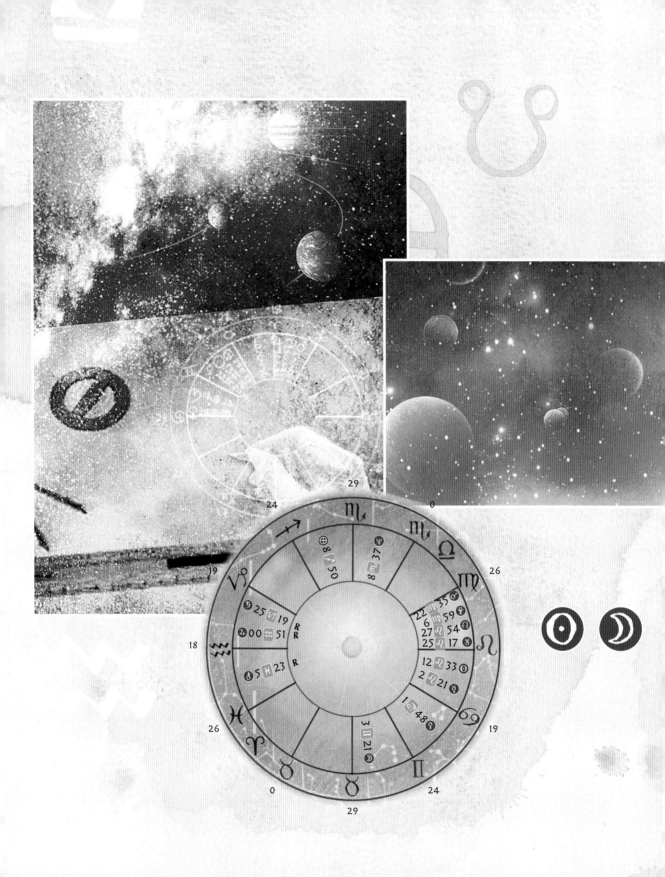

CHAPTER 5
CYCLES, RETURNS, AND TRANSITS

Each person's data—date, place, and time of birth—yields
a unique horoscope or "nativity." Think of this as a photograph
of the heavens that captures the position of the planets and
angles at the precise moment of birth and as seen from the
precise location on planet Earth. Natal interpretation, as
illustrated in this book so far, is based on this one frozen
moment in time. After your moment of birth, the planets, of
course, continue on their way. Predictive astrology therefore
approaches the horoscope as a mechanism in perpetual
motion, which symbolizes the unfolding and development
of the individual's life and purpose.

PREDICTION: SETTING THE CHART IN MOTION

Prediction is based on the astronomical fact that the heavens are in constant motion and on the astrological symbolic principle of "as above, so below." In some awesome and wondrous way, the planets' journeys are simply reflecting our own. Looking into this vast cosmic mirror tells us what has already happened (retrodiction), what is happening now, and what is unfolding for the future (prediction).

Think of the heavens as a busy railway junction. Signal boxes are constantly at work with red or green lights flashing as some trains zip through at speed on their way to distant destinations, while others travel to smaller neighborhoods nearby. Some slow down to stop, to pick up passengers, and then move off again. Some stop at their terminus and then do the same journey in reverse, others get delayed, while yet others move in and out of different platforms—all in a masterminded, synchronized production. It is a never-sleeping picture of many moving parts, making up a perfectly orchestrated whole. As to whether you can expect a "good" or a "bad" day/week/month/year depends on which train you are on and why.

UNIVERSAL

Here we find the stuff of Sun-sign columns. If I am writing for the media or preparing my blog, the task is to locate and interpret the current activity. This includes:

Through which signs the planets are currently traveling

The aspects these planets are making to each other

INGRESSES
when a planet is changing sign, such as from Cancer into Leo, and therefore opening a new cycle

LUNATIONS
New and full Moons, and eclipses (also vital for personal charts, see p. 144)

STATIONS
when planets are switching from direct to retrograde motion, or vice versa, and marking crossroads

PARTICULAR

Comparing the perpetual motion of the planets to the "frozen moment" of the nativity forms the basis of an astrologer's predictions. It is here that we enter the exciting world of "transits"—pinpointing the moments when any transiting (traveling) planet aligns with any of the natal (stationary) planets or angles.

A book called the Ephemerides is the astrologer's bible. I never go anywhere without mine. This is like a huge railway timetable (the one I am currently using is from 1920 to 2020, a month to a page), detailing the journeys of the planets for every single day. There are ten columns on each page, one for each of the traditional planets, Sun through to Pluto, and the rows of figures give you the exact degree/sign/minute of the planets, starting at midnight of each day (a 0h Ephemerides) or at midday of each day (a noon Ephemerides).

Consulting your Ephemerides enables you to plan your way ahead or to look at the journeys you have already made. You can find where any planet was/is/will be at any given time. Make sure you buy an Ephemerides that includes the all-important Aspectarian—the exact times for all the aspects being made each day and between which planets.

CYCLES AND TRANSITS

Each planet travels through the 12 signs of the zodiac at a different speed (see chart, opposite). The "personal" planets, Sun through to Saturn, take from between a year to nearly 30 years to make a full lap of the zodiac (Aries to Pisces), whereas the cycles of the outer or "generational" planets are significantly slower.

When we translate this into "daily motion"—how far a planet moves from midnight to the next midnight or midday to the next midday—this means that the Sun moves 1 degree a day. Apart from the Sun and the Moon, all the other planets spend periods of time in the year in retrograde motion, meaning that they appear to spend several weeks or months moving backwards. Thus their speed is always variable rather than constant, but Mercury and Venus average 1 degree a day, and Mars averages about half a degree a day.

The remaining planets all move much more slowly. Even at full speed Jupiter will travel no more than 7 degrees in an entire month, and the other planets do no more than inch their way backwards and forwards, frequently covering less than 1 or 2 degrees in a month.

As each planet moves around the horoscope at its own speed, it will transit— cross over—the degrees (exact positions) of the other planets in the chart. At this stage, the importance of knowing your aspects comes into its own as a transiting planet aligns with a natal planet when it reaches the same degree. In exactly the same way as identifying natal aspects, the number of signs apart determines the aspect being made.

For example, let us say that your natal Sun is at 5 degrees of Leo. Consulting the Ephemerides we can see that:
* Jupiter ingress Leo on July 16, 2014
* Jupiter reached 5 degrees of Leo on August 8, 2014
* Therefore Jupiter transited the Sun by conjunction on this date

As we now know that Jupiter has a 12-year cycle, it follows that the last time Jupiter transited the Sun by conjunction would have been in 2002. Consulting the Ephemerides, we find that Jupiter was at 5 degrees of Leo at the end of August 2002.

Further, we also know that Jupiter would have transited the Sun by opposition in the middle of these two dates, when he was roughly halfway through his 12-year journey. Again, consulting the Ephemerides we find:
* Jupiter ingress Aquarius on January 5, 2009
* Jupiter reached 5 degrees of Aquarius on January 26, 2009
* Therefore Jupiter transited the Sun by opposition on this date

You can do the same exercise for all the planets and also for the other major aspects—the squares, trines, and sextiles—but the conjunctions and oppositions are by far the most important.

HOW LONG DOES A TRANSIT LAST?

The Sun will transit each of the other planets and the four angles within the course of a year, but, because the Sun moves so quickly—by a degree a day—these transits last only for a day, and the same applies to Mercury and Venus. As Mars has a two-year cycle, his transits last for two days. These contacts are therefore not usually significant in terms of major life events or changes but tend to operate on a more mundane, day-to-day level, reflecting their own symbolism. It is not within the scope of this book to offer interpretations for all the possible planetary combinations but, as a rough guide, Mercury transits link to communication, such as news, a decision, an idea, an e-mail, and so on; Venus transits signal key dates for love, beauty, pleasure, and money issues; and Mars transits indicate emotional matters relating to anger, action, energy, friction, or sex.

The last five traditional planets, Jupiter to Pluto, and also Chiron, take many months to transit a particular degree and, therefore, the other natal planets, and are thus the harbingers of change in terms of indicating major life events. Their transits reflect their own symbolism, as illustrated in the remainder of this chapter.

PLANET		DIGNITY
☉	Sun	1 year
☽	Moon	28 days
☿	Mercury	1 year
♀	Venus	1 year
♂	Mars	2 years
♃	Jupiter	12 years
♄	Saturn	29½ years
♅	Uranus	84 years
♆	Neptune	176 years
♇	Pluto	248 years
⚷	Chiron	51 year

Note

Transits will be for good or ill depending on the nature of the transiting planet, the condition of the natal one, and whether the transit is being formed by a harmonious or inharmonious aspect. The example opposite would be considered highly fortunate with Jupiter, planet of luck and opportunity, conjuncting the Sun in Leo, his sign of dignity. The opposition would also signal positive events, but probably in more challenging circumstances.

RETURNS

A planet's "return" means the moment when it comes full circle. For example, when the Sun completes his year's cycle, he will be back at the same degree and minute of the same sign as found in the natal chart. This is called the Solar Return and marks our birthday (many happy returns of the day).

Mercury and Venus returns also happen once a year and Mars returns happen once every two years. These dates usually mark minor but nonetheless significant landmarks on our life journeys, relating to the nature of the planet's natal condition—that is, the planet's sign, house, and aspects.

THE MOON

The Moon is the swiftest moving body and needs to be treated as a separate factor. She whizzes through the zodiac every twenty-eight days, spending approximately two and a half days in each sign. Every two weeks we have a new or full Moon, commonly known as lunations.

NEW MOON

When the Moon is exactly conjunct the Sun, so they are always in the same sign. The opening of a new cycle, the point at which something is born, associated with beginnings, fertility, sowing seeds, and making fresh starts.

FULL MOON

When the Moon is exactly opposite the Sun, receiving all his light, so they are always in opposite signs. The completion of a cycle, associated with recognition, achievement, and illumination. It is notoriously a time of "lunacy," as anyone working in the health and safety professions will tell you.

However, the slower moving the planet, the more important the "return," so, again, our major life shifts and events correlate more with the outer planets (Jupiter to Pluto and Chiron) than with the personal ones (Sun to Mars).

In terms of predictive power, lunations are important if they fall in the same sign and within a few degrees (the tighter the orb, the more potent the contact) of a natal planet or angle. This is like the heavens taking a highlighter pen to that planet or angle, either for an isolated event or, more usually, as a "testimony" to a transit already in operation, adding extra weight to an interpretation already taking shape.

Lunations also assist greatly with timing. The important transits are at work for many months at a time, but lunations happen every two weeks and therefore pinpoint a window of time that is especially sensitive. For example, if a major transit signals the start of a new relationship, also look for a relevant lunation, such as one that falls:
- Conjunct the Ascendant or Descendant
- In aspect to planets in the 7th house or ruler of the 7th house
- In aspect to Venus or Mars as universal signifiers of romance

A lunation on one of these relevant points could narrow down the time scale from a matter of months to a couple of weeks on either side of the lunation.

ECLIPSES

Eclipses are even more notable in terms of sensitizing an astrological picture in the making.

A Solar Eclipse occurs when the Sun is obscured by the shadow of the Moon at the time of a new Moon

A Lunar Eclipse occurs when the Moon is obscured by the shadow of the earth at the time of a full Moon

Eclipses are often considered as "power points" in a developing situation but they have a tricky side, too. Look for the symbolism of being overshadowed by another, a light going out, or power battles in triangular matters, such as affairs. You will find examples of lunations and eclipses in the following sections.

TRANSITS OF THE MAJOR PLANETS

JUPITER

Jupiter transits signal the possibility for: Expansion, foreign travel, emigration, higher education, opportunity, good fortune, litigation, liberation, acclaim, faith in oneself or in another, events unfolding easily and propitiously, the arrival of those who are a blessing, who are inspirational, generous, helpful or good for us.

There is no better way to start learning about transits and returns than by looking at your own horoscope, simply because you know about your own life better than anyone else's. Check the following cycles against your own history and you will find that events will reflect the symbolism of the planet in question. Studying the charts of well-known people who interest you is also highly educational as their life stories, along with precise dates, are usually public information, as illustrated in the celebrity anecdotes in the following sections.

With a 12-year cycle, Jupiter returns are the most frequent of the major planets and we all experience these returns roughly at the ages of 12, 24, 36, 48, and so on. We can expect events of a Jupiterian nature to unfold at these times. These returns will be especially significant for the Jupiter-ruled signs (Sagittarius or Pisces) or if Jupiter is prominently placed in the horoscope.

Throughout his 12-year-cycle, Jupiter will transit all the other planets and angles of the chart. Whatever the particular details may be, Jupiter's general principle is to move us on, encouraging us to think big, and widen our horizons in every possible sense.

BARACK AND MICHELLE OBAMA

Barack Obama (b. August 4, 1961) was sworn in as the 44th president of the United States on January 20, 2009, within two weeks of his fourth Jupiter return.

- Jupiter ingress Aquarius January 5, 2009
- Obama's Jupiter Return 0.51 Aquarius January 9, 2009

As a Democrat and the first African American to hold the office, it is symbolically appropriate that Jupiter, planet of the free, should be the most active planet in his chart at this time. Furthermore, his natal Jupiter is stronger than he might look at first:

- Jupiter in his natural house of the 12th
- Conjunct Saturn the chart ruler (this is a "dissociate" aspect, that is, although

Saturn is in the previous sign of Capricorn, the two planets are still less than 8 degrees apart and are therefore said to make a dissociate conjunction).

- The Mercury-Jupiter opposition is "mediated" (helped out) by both being in good aspect to the Moon in Mercury's sign of Gemini (Moon sextile Mercury, trine Jupiter). Obama is especially praised for his powers of oratory.

The symbolism of Jupiter in Aquarius, sign of the collective and socialism, was reflected in the theme of the inaugural speech, "A New Birth of Freedom," in which he called upon Americans to recognize shared responsibility. Jupiter's placing in the 12th house of Obama's chart— suffering, places of confinement, such as prisons or hospitals— was also apparent in his objectives of establishing affordable health care for all Americans.

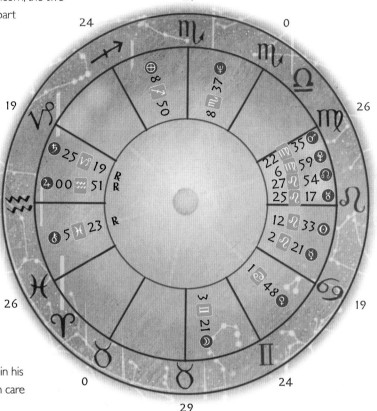

BARACK OBAMA

4 AUGUST 1961
19:24
HONOLULU

The lunation prior to the inauguration date was a full Moon on January 11 at 21 Cancer, opposite Obama's Saturn, the ruling planet of his chart.

The following lunation was a new Moon that was also a Solar Eclipse on January 26, at 6 Aquarius, conjunct his Jupiter.

On the day of the inauguration, which was almost exactly in the middle of the two lunations, the Sun was conjunct Mercury at just under 1 degree of Aquarius, and therefore exactly conjunct Obama's Jupiter.

I have no recorded birth time for Michelle Obama (b. January 17, 1964), but her chart is brilliant for illustrating a Jupiter transit at a universal level, and an example of how accurate astrology can be even if you do not have a precise birth time and you are using a noon chart (as suggested in the introduction to Chapter One) instead.

- Michelle Obama was born January 17, 1964 in Chicago.
- Mars is at 3 degrees of Aquarius throughout January 17.
- A noon chart would give her a natal Mars of 3.32 Aquarius.

The new presidential term starts at noon on the inauguration day, which put transiting Jupiter at 3.33 Aquarius, exactly conjunct her natal Mars, a fabulous and precise symbolic showing for the moment her husband (Mars as universal significator for men) became president.

SATURN

Saturn transits signal the possibility for: Work, effort, ambition, setting goals, responsibility, limitations, restrictions, frustration, illness, bereavement, events unfolding slowly or wishes being denied, the arrival of those who are of professional value to us, those with whom we develop a serious relationship, or with whom we feel a karmic connection.

With his cycle of 29½ years, the first Saturn return happens during the run-up to our 30th birthday. This is a hugely formative time and is commonly referred to as the astrological coming of age. Suddenly we are not going to be 20-something anymore, a sobering clock is ticking, and we sense the importance of getting our life in order. We can expect events of a Saturnian nature to unfold at this time.

Make or break is a strong theme. Many people "settle down" under the first Saturn return, through commitment either to marriage or a career, or both. Conversely, relationships that are not working come to an end, especially between couples who married young and who find at this stage that they have outgrown each other.

The second Saturn return happens at roughly age 59, often coinciding with plans for or actual retirement. Saturn's third cycle marks the beginning of the journey into old age. These returns will be especially significant for the Saturn-ruled signs (Capricorn and Aquarius) or if Saturn is prominently placed in the horoscope.

Throughout his 29½-year cycle, Saturn will transit all the other planets and angles of the chart. Whatever the particular details may be, Saturn's general principle is to bring maturity, realism, awareness of limitations, acceptance of responsibility, strength through endurance, and solid results for our efforts.

THE DUKE AND DUCHESS OF CAMBRIDGE
The marriage of Prince William (b. June 21, 1982) to Kate Middleton (b. January 9, 1982) is textbook Saturn return stuff. We have no official time of birth for Kate, but this does not change Saturn's position of 21.50 Libra, the sign of partnership and Saturn's sign of exaltation. We cannot know Saturn's position by house, but we can say that, as a Capricorn, the Saturn return would be an especially important time for Kate.

At the end of January 1982 Saturn turned retrograde, so that by the time William was born, Saturn had backtracked to 15.30 Libra. In fact, his Saturn is "stationary direct," as Saturn switched from retrograde to direct on June 18, marking this planet as especially powerful. As William's Saturn is 6 degrees before Kate's, this means that, although Kate is five months older than William, he, in fact, reached his Saturn return first, the cycle being exact from mid-December 2010 to the beginning of September 2011. The wedding took place in the middle of these two dates on April 29, 2011.

Kate's Saturn return was exact in October 2011, six months into her marriage and her new life as a working royal. It was later reported that by October, Kate was researching the charities for which she would become patron, and that in this same month she had written to nine-year-old Fabian Bate, a child with leukemia, whom she had visited at the Royal Marsden Hospital, praising him for his strength. When her charity list was decided, it was announced that Kate would be the Royal Patron of East Anglia's Children's Hospices, thus echoing the Saturn link to death and the dying.

ELIN NORDEGREN

The more difficult face to Saturn plays out in endings. We have no birth time for another Capricorn, Elin Nordegren (b. January 1, 1980), ex-wife of Tiger Woods, but with natal Saturn at 27 Virgo, she experienced her Saturn return from October 2009 to May 2010, when Saturn went "stationary direct" at 27.50 Virgo at the very end of that month. It was November 2009 when the Woods scandal hit the press and Elin discovered the full extent of his infidelities. By the end of the year, Woods had entered rehab for sex addiction but Elin allegedly did not decide to leave him until the following April, when a mistress too many came to light. In that month the lunar testimonies were:

- April 14, 2010: New Moon at 24 Aries (self) opposite her natal Pluto (finality) at 21 Libra (partnership)
- April 28, 2010: Full Moon at 8 Scorpio (sex and secrets coming to light) opposite her natal Chiron (the wound) at 9 Taurus

Chiron in Taurus (money) is part of a tight grand trine in earth signs, including the Sun at 10 Capricorn (fellow Capricorn husband) and Jupiter (good fortune) at 10 Virgo.

Owing to the absence of a recorded time of birth, we cannot know the actual house position of her natal planets, but I would speculate that one of these planets is in or ruler of the 8th house, domain of sex and also the partner's money. Their divorce settlement was one of the largest in history.

PRINCE WILLIAM

21 JUNE 1982
21:03 BST
LONDON

TRANSITS OF THE OUTER PLANETS

URANUS

Uranus transits signal the possibility for: Drama, sudden change, disruption, impulsivity, the unexpected, rebellion, shocks or surprises, events that come like a bolt out of the blue, the arrival of those who knock us off balance, who challenge our views, sweep us off our feet, or turn our world upside down.

Note
Uranus is erratic in nature and also has an erratic orbit, so the midpoint of his journey falls anywhere between the ages of 38 and 42. This is called the Uranus half return, commonly referred to as the astrological midlife crisis. Some area of life is restructured, sometimes dramatically, and often this manifests as a claiming of something unlived up until this point, a sense of "if I don't do it now, I never will." Divorces, marriages, and "last-chance" babies are incredibly common at this time.

Now that we have reached the slow-moving outer planets, we enter the realm of increasingly long cycles. Any transits of Uranus (up to the age of 84), Neptune, or Pluto (and now we also include the modern-day Chiron) are "one offs," and therefore score high on the scale of symbolic importance. Also, these transits can last many months, owing to the fact that they spend long periods of time in retrograde motion, making a "backwards and forwards" journey rather than a continuous one.

As he makes his 84-year lap, Uranus will eventually cross over all the other planets and angles, but it is his halfway point that is especially important. For example, if natal Uranus is at 4 degrees of Libra, then Uranus will have reached his halfway point when he arrives at 4 degrees of Aries.

Either side of the half return we will, of course, experience Uranus's transits to the other planets and angles, and his general principle is the "wake-up call" to bring progress, social advancement, to shake us out of complacency and to embrace the experimental, to break the mold rather than staying in a rut or clinging to convention. We all experience Uranus's shockwaves in one guise or another, but his transits and the half return are often especially significant for Aquarians or if Uranus is prominently placed in the horoscope.

ELLEN DEGENERES
Ellen DeGeneres (b. January 26, 1958) is a powerful Aquarian in both these respects. She has a triple conjunction in this sign of the Sun, Venus, and Chiron, all opposing Uranus in Leo. Note that this puts the Sun and Uranus in "mutual reception," that is, the relationship between the two planets is strengthened by the fact that they occupy each other's signs. They are able to "swap over," lifting each other out of detriment and into dignity.

- Uranus entered Aquarius in January 1996 and transited:
  - Conjunct her Sun from February to December 1997
  - Conjunct her Venus (love, women, sex) and opposite to his own natal placing— the half return—from February to December 1998

The increasing urge to go public about her sexual orientation is astrologically crystal clear. Uranus starting his transit over her Sun (identity) lit a fuse that was inextinguishable and Ellen "came out" in February 1997 on *The Oprah Winfrey Show*. In April, her own character in *Ellen*, her sitcom with ABC Television, followed suit:

- April 7, 1997, new Moon at 17.40 Aries, almost exactly conjunct Ellen's own natal Moon of 17.10 Aries (sign of self). On April 14 she appeared on the front cover of *Time* magazine under the banner, "Yep, I'm Gay."
- Her relationship with Anne Heche (b. May 25, 1969) started hot on the heels of this publicity. Note that Anne's Descendant is 19 Aries with Venus at 21 Aries, both conjunct Ellen's Moon, and therefore also being highlighted by the new Moon. To add to the theme, Anne's natal Uranus of 29 Virgo is conjunct Ellen's Part of Fortune at 27 Virgo.

The news was far more explosive than she could have predicted. Being the source of media frenzy is apt Uranus symbolism and the ensuing controversy led to ABC's eventual axing of her show in May 1998; her career temporarily nose-dived. As a true Uranian, however, she bounced back and *The Ellen DeGeneres Show* was launched on September 8, 2003, under the propitious auspices of a Jupiter transit. It was the beginning of a stupendous comeback.

ELLEN DEGENERES

26 JANUARY 1958
03:00
METAIRIE, LA

Note

Her natal Venus–Uranus opposition has an orb of only 9 minutes of arc, making this the tightest aspect in her chart. In psychological terms, Uranus rules dissociation, the "split" in all of us, the part of our psyche that disowns or denies all that is uncomfortable or undesirable. This is reflected in mythology as Uranus was castrated by his son Chronos (Saturn), and his severed genitals were cast into the sea. Venus (feminine identity and sexuality) opposite Uranus is clearly the symbolic "signature" in Ellen's chart for being gay.

NEPTUNE

Neptune transits signal the possibility for: Confusion, uncertainty, delusion, illusion, deception, soul searching, a lack of purpose or direction, being "all at sea," grief, events that make no logical sense, escapism, mystical experiences, and all issues related to altered states of consciousness, including anesthesia, all drugs and alcohol, surrender, sacrifice, the arrival of those who mesmerize, manipulate, or idealize us, those we want to rescue or vice versa, or with whom we feel a spiritual connection.

With a cycle of 176 years, none of us will ever experience a Neptune return, and even the half return will not happen until we are well into our 80s. You can, however, note the quarter return, when he is square to his natal position, which happens in the early 40s. This event and all Neptune transits will be especially significant for Pisceans or if Neptune is prominently placed in the horoscope.

As Neptune's journey is so slow, his transits, when they happen, are usually of great importance. From the above possibilities you will see that mostly these transits are not easy. The planet of all things marine brings sea changes and sea mists, foggy situations in which all the edges are blurred and nothing is as it seems. It is like looking at the world through a rainy window. At worst, with Neptune's connection to the 12th house, the Vale of Tears, these transits can signal times of very real suffering for which keywords such as "confusion" or "uncertainty" are hopelessly inadequate. Neptune's waves can be engulfing and nothing swamps you like grief does.

GEORGE CLOONEY

6 MAY 1961
02:58
LEXINGTON MANOR (KY), USA

THE ASTROLOGICAL TIMELINE

September 2013
The new Moon at 13.04 Virgo falls conjunct George's Descendant (partnership angle). George and Amal start dating

April 29, 2014
The new Moon, also a solar eclipse at 8.52 Taurus, falls opposite George's natal Neptune at 9.48, less than 24 hours after the engagement

August 2014
The second transit of Neptune over Chiron. George and Amal post their wedding bans at Chelsea Town Hall, London, UK

At best, Neptunian times can be idyllic. Whereas Uranus shocks or divides, Neptune dissolves and seeks fusion, collapsing our personal boundaries, without which we would never experience true empathy, falling in love, or mystical enlightenment. For a while we know ultimate unity—that perfect "oneness"—with another or with the universe. It is learning how to separate again and how to replace the boundaries, to distinguish between infatuation and authentic love, which defines the Neptunian struggle.

GEORGE CLOONEY

As mentioned previously, Neptune is frequently a powerful player in the horoscopes of actors. George Clooney may be an earthy Taurus, but he has a Pisces Ascendant, a Sun–Neptune (co-ruler) opposition, and Jupiter (chart ruler) in square to Neptune. In his personal life, with one brief marriage that ended in 1993 and strings of short-lived relationships, he has been known as one of the world's most eligible bachelors. This role came to an end with his engagement to Amal Alamuddin (b. February 3, 1978).

March 2014
Neptune (co-ruler as he has a Pisces Ascendant) starts transiting conjunct natal Chiron at 6.08 Pisces and opposite natal Pluto at 5.34 Virgo

April 28, 2014
The engagement is announced

September 9, 2014
Right on cue, the full Moon at 16.19 Pisces falls conjunct George's Ascendant, the very day that he publicly states that the wedding will take place in Italy within the next couple of weeks. The full Moon lighting up the Ascendant also often signals personal recognition. Less than a week later, it is announced that George would be receiving the Cecil B. DeMille Award, presented annually to an individual who has made an incredible impact on the world of entertainment, at the 2015 Golden Globe Awards on January 11, 2015—just two weeks before the third and final transit of Neptune over Chiron.

PLUTO

Pluto transit signals: Total change, endings, loss, absence, disempowerment, depression, "death and rebirth" processes, events that are overwhelming or that are taken out of our hands, the arrival of those who fascinate or control us, or for whom we give everything up in order to start a new life.

With his cycle of 248 years, none of us can even experience Pluto's half return, but we can note the quarter return, when he is square to his natal position. Pluto has an erratic orbit so you will need to check the Ephemerides for the exact dates, but as a rough guide the aspect of Pluto square Pluto follows this time frame:

- Born 1940, transit at age 44
- Born 1950, transit at age 40
- Born 1960, transit at age 36
- Born 1970, transit at age 36
- Born 1980, transit at age 39
- Born 1990, transit at age 43

This event and all Pluto transits will be especially significant for Scorpios or if Pluto is prominently placed in the horoscope.

When it comes to change, Pluto has no equal. Saturn is hard work, Uranus explodes, Neptune dissolves, but Pluto annihilates. His job is to demolish, and when he has finished, he slams the door behind him, leaving us to start again from scratch.

Astrological literature has latched on to the word "transformation" for Pluto, but this can fall drastically short of describing the Plutonic experience, which is usually a long and painful process and most definitely not the wave of a magic wand. Pluto is god of the underworld, and Pluto transits can, at their worst, be a trip to hell and back as one way of life "dies" in order for the new to be born. The word "transformative" is nearer to the mark as we grapple with Pluto's uncompromising nature and "all or nothing" experiences.

JENNIFER ANISTON

Jennifer (b. February 11, 1969) has a strongly placed Pluto in her natal chart. At 24.32 Virgo, Pluto is in very tight aspect to three of her personal planets and the Ascendant/Descendant horizon:

- A very close sextile to Mars, ruler of the 7th house of marriage, at 23.50 in Pluto's sign of Scorpio
- Quinqunx her Sun at 23.22 Aquarius
- Square her Moon 23.15 Sagittarius

- Semi-sextile her Ascendant and quinqunx her Descendant

Her marriage to Brad Pitt broke down when he was going through his Uranus half return and she was suffering the devastation of Pluto transiting conjunct her Moon (emotional needs, the other woman), a transit that lasted from January to November 2005. Brad and Angelina (b. June 4, 1975) met on the set of *Mr. and Mrs, Smith* in the summer of 2004, but note that Jennifer's exact Pluto transit kicks in as the moment of finality (Pluto) is confirmed.

- January 7, 2005: Jennifer and Brad's separation is announced and she files for divorce two months later.
- October 2, 2005: The divorce is finalized as Pluto approaches Jennifer's Moon for the third and final time.
- October 3, 2005: Symbolically this is confirmed within 24 hours with a new Moon that is also a solar eclipse at 10.19 Libra, falling exactly opposite:
  - Jennifer's natal Venus (chart ruler) at 9.14 Aries
  - Brad's natal Jupiter (chart ruler) at 9.50 Aries
  - Angelina's natal Mars at 10.43 Aries
- October17, 2005: The following full Moon, which is also a lunar eclipse at 24.13 Aries falls exactly conjunct:
  - Jennifer's Descendant 24.29 Aries
  - Angelina Jolie's natal Chiron at 26.46 Aries (see Angelina Jolie's chart, p. 134)

Pluto transits themselves often signal triangular situations and the inevitable power struggles these can reflect. Here, the eclipse symbolism underlines Pluto's finale; Angelina would have been about one month into her first pregnancy in October and there is no going back.

SELF-DESTRUCTION AND DEPRESSION

Pluto transits are also huge warning signs of self-destructive behavior or for those on the "at risk" register of depression, especially when transiting by opposition or square, and particularly when involving the chart ruler or natal planets in a weakened state.

Philip Seymour Hoffman (July 23, 1967–February 2, 2014) died of a drug overdose. Transiting Pluto was in his 8th house at 12.20 Capricorn, exactly opposite his natal Mercury (chart ruler as he had a Gemini Ascendant) at 12.37 Cancer and square his natal Saturn at 12.28 Aries (sign of fall).

Robin Williams tragically committed suicide on August 11, 2014. Transiting Pluto (chart co-ruler as he had a Scorpio Ascendant) was at 11.25 Capricorn, exactly opposite his natal Uranus at 10.51 Cancer, which is conjunct natal Mars (chart ruler in his sign of fall) at 11.56 Cancer, both posited in the 8th house. The natal Mars/Uranus conjunction is the outlet to a cardinal T-Square, the other two planets being the opposition of Jupiter and Neptune. What had shown as a zany, whacky, and often uncontainable humor of a comic genius in life also ended up as the escape route from an unbearable suffering of his human spirit.

CHIRON

Chiron transits signal the possibility for: Emotional wounding, anguish, learning experiences for personal and spiritual growth, finding or giving guidance, evolving own beliefs, healing old hurts, events that unfold in a subtle but meaningful or magical way, the arrival of those who can teach us with their wisdom or heal us with their skills and compassion.

Chiron has a highly eccentric orbit, so you will need to check the Ephemerides for exactitude, especially for the dates of the half return, but the Chiron return itself happens at around the age of 50. Until that moment, Chiron will transit all the other planets and angles of the chart, signaling events related to the above issues. These are likely to be especially significant for those who have Chiron prominently placed in their horoscope.

BRITNEY SPEARS

Britney Spears (b. December 2, 1981) has Chiron at 19.23 Taurus in her 8th house, in the awkward quinqunx to her 1st house Saturn at 19.17 Libra, and square to her Moon in Aquarius in her 5th house of children. This alignment speaks of emotional difficulties that caught up with her in early 2007. On January 21, her aunt, to whom she was very close, died of ovarian cancer, and on February 16, she publicly shaved her head, which could have been a cry for help or a deliberate ploy to prevent her hair from being analyzed for drugs. Either way, it was followed by visits to rehab centers, setting the stage for Chiron's transit conjunct her Moon throughout 2007:

- Chiron conjunct her Moon for the first time in March. On March 29, 2007, five months after Britney filed for divorce, a settlement with Kevin Federline is reached.
- Chiron turns retrograde in May, her divorce is finalized in July.
- Chiron conjunct her Moon for the second time in August, when Federline seeks primary physical custody of their two children.
- In September, Britney is ordered to undergo random drug and alcohol testing twice a week and both parents are ordered to refrain from drinking and using drugs around their children.
- Chiron turns direct again in October. Britney is told that she must surrender custody of her children to her ex-husband and, at the end of the month, she is granted three monitored visits a week with her sons.
- Chiron conjunct her Moon for the third and final time in December. The custody battle is at its most painful and an attorney from the Los Angeles County Department of Children and Family Services reports concerns about the safety and welfare of the two toddlers if left in their mother's care.

This sequence of events led to her being hospitalized in January 2008. Federline was awarded sole custody of their sons and Britney's visitation rights were suspended. It was a long, slow, and painful collapse that played out through the main concerns of the 5th house—not only the impact on her children but exposing the wounds from her own childhood. Her status reverted to child as she was placed under her father's conservatorship, whereby he took complete control of all her assets for her own protection and well-being at that time.

ELLEN AND PORTIA

As stated in the Uranus section, Ellen DeGeneres (see her chart p. 151) has a triple conjunction of the Sun, Venus, and Chiron in Aquarius. Her civil partner Portia de Rossi (b. January 31, 1973) also has a Sagittarius Ascendant and is a fellow Aquarian. Her Sun at 10.38 Aquarius is conjunct Mercury (ruler of 7th house) at 11.56 Aquarius. This conjunction therefore falls conjunct Ellen's Venus at 9.55 Aquarius, a perfect showing of "synastry"— astrological compatibility.

Ellen's Chiron return lasted from February to November 2008. She and Portia were married in the middle of this cycle, on August 16, 2008:

- Transiting Jupiter (chart ruler) at 13 Capricorn, conjunct Ellen's Mercury (ruler of 7th).
- The lunation prior to the event was a new Moon that was also a solar eclipse at 9.32 Leo, so conjunct Ellen's Uranus at 9.46 Leo and opposite her Venus.
- The next lunation fell on August 16, the wedding day itself, a full Moon that was also a lunar eclipse at 24.21 Aquarius, exactly sextile Portia's Ascendant of 24.23 Sagittarius.

There are obvious Aquarius/Uranus themes in play at the time of the Chiron return, underlining the powerful connection between the emotional fracturing of the Uranus half return and the healing and fulfillment of a legalized wedding in the eyes of the world a decade later. This was a major landmark for Ellen personally, but also universally in terms of her role as educator, there being a direct link between a society's level of civilization and its level of tolerance to same-sex relationships.

BRITNEY SPEARS

2 DECEMBER 1981
01:30
KENTWOOD, LA

INDEX

ACKNOWLEDGMENTS

As with the completion of every creative project there are many thanks owing:

To my twin sister Sue Rossides, who read every single word of this book before it went to print. Your constructive criticism led to countless little revisions that made the whole so much better. Thank you from my heart for all the times you set aside your own concerns to read, discuss, and encourage, and for your faith and unconditional love that enriches my life every single day.

To my brother-in-law Mike Rossides who also gave endless support, who knows absolutely nothing about astrology but who never doubted for one moment my ability to write this book.

To my very first publisher and now friend Denise Brown who decided out of the blue to introduce me to Cico Books—the rest, as they say, is history.

To friend and colleague Sally Kirkman for all the early discussions that helped to craft the focus of this book, especially in relation to the cameos of celebrities.

To friend and fellow astrologer Ingrid Hoffman, whose constant flow of loving, insightful, and uplifting emails winging their way from Cape Town sustained me in my creative journey and often kept me on track with my ideas and message.

To astrologer Melanie Reinhart whose generous input into the Chiron section was invaluable.

To everyone at Cico Books, notably editors Lauren Mulholland whose sensitive, enthusiastic, and intelligent handling of all the material, from day one, ensured that this book turned out as originally envisaged but better, and Dawn Bates who expertly picked up the reins midfield.

To copy-editor Jennifer Jahn who made exactly the right input and Sarah Perkins whose specially commissioned vivid artwork brought these pages to life.

To the website Astrotheme without whose staggeringly detailed database of celebrities this book could not have been written in this form.

To all my family, friends, clients, and students for your enthusiasm, support, and permission to use your stories.

Most importantly, in loving memory of my beloved and so deeply missed friend Paul "Chippy" Johnson who passed over in the middle of writing this book.

BIBLIOGRAPHY, RESOURCES, AND RECOMMENDED FURTHER READING

- *Astrology for Beginners*, Maggie Hyde and Geoffrey Cornelius. Icon Books Ltd, Penguin Group, Cambridge, 1995
- Astrotheme.com – website of data for celebrity horoscopes
- *Chiron and the Healing Journey: an Astrological and Psychological Perspective*, Melanie Reinhart. Starwalker Press, 2010
- *Christian Astrology*, William Lilly. Regulus Publishing Co Ltd, 1985
- *Eclipses – the Power Points of Astrology*, Derek Appleby and Maurice McCann. The Aquarian Press, Wellingborough Northamptonshire, 1986
- *Horary Astrology Rediscovered*, Olivia Barclay. Whitford Press, Schiffer Publishing Ltd, Pennsylvania, 1990
- *Jung and Astrology*, Maggie Hyde. The Aquarian Press, London, 1992
- *The Karmic Journey – The Birthchart, Karma and Reincarnation*, Judy Hall. Arkana, Penguin Group London, 1990
- *The Moment of Astrology*, Geoffrey Cornelius. Arkana Penguin Books, London, 1994
- *The Principles of Astrology* – Charles E. O. Carter. The Theosophical Publishing House, Wheaton III. USA, 1963
- *Profiles of Women*, Lois M Rodden. The American Federation of Astrologers, Inc. USA, 1979
- *Relating*, Liz Greene. The Aquarian Press, Wellingborough Northamptonshire, 1986
- *Saturn, a New Look at an Old Devil*, Liz Greene. Samuel Weiser, Inc. York Beach, Maine, 1976
- *Secrets from a Stargazer's Notebook*, Debbi Kempton Smith. Bantam Books, USA, 1982